McDougal Littell

Geometry

Concepts and Skills

Larson   Boswell   Stiff

Notetaking Guide

The Notetaking Guide contains a lesson-by-lesson
framework that allows students to take notes on and
review the main concepts of each lesson in the textbook.
Each Notetaking Guide lesson features worked-out
examples, Follow-Up exercises and Checkpoint
exercises. Each example has a number of write-on lines
for students to complete, either in class as the example is
discussed or at home as part of a review of the lesson.
Each chapter concludes with a review of the main
vocabulary of the chapter. Upon completion, each
chapter of the Notetaking Guide can be used by students
to help review for the test on that particular chapter.

D1717078

McDougal Littell

A HOUGHTON MIFFLIN COMPANY

Evanston, Illinois • Boston • Dallas

Contents

Geometry Concepts and Skills Notetaking Guide

Contents

Geometry, Concepts and Skills
Notetaking Guide

Copyright © Mc
a division of Houghton Mi

Contents

Contents

1.1 Finding and Describing Patterns

Goal Find patterns and use them to make predictions.

Example 1 *Describe a Visual Pattern*

Describe a pattern in the figures.

Solution

Notice that the number of sides increases. Write the number of sides each figure has. Look for a pattern.

___   ___   ___   ___

Answer The number of sides increases by ____.

Follow-Up

Make up your own visual pattern and describe it.

Example 2   *Describe a Number Pattern*

Describe a pattern in the numbers.

a. 3, 6, 9, 12, 15, 18, ...   b. 1, 4, 9, 16, 25, 36, ...

Solution

a. Notice that the numbers increase. Find the difference between each number and the previous number.

     First pair: $6 - 3 = $ ___

     Second pair: $9 - 6 = $ ___

     Third pair: ___ $-$ ___ $=$ ___

     Fourth pair: ___ $-$ ___ $=$ ___

     Fifth pair: ___ $-$ ___ $=$ ___

Answer Each number is ___ more than the previous number.

b. Notice that the numbers are perfect squares. For each number in the pattern, write the number that is squared.

Pattern	1	4	9	16	25	36
Number Squared	$(\_\_)^2$	$(\_\_)^2$	$(\_\_)^2$	$(\_\_)^2$	$(\_\_)^2$	$(\_\_)^2$

Answer The numbers are _____ of the counting numbers 1, 3, 4, 5, 6, ...

Follow-Up

If the numbers in a pattern increase, must they increase by a constant amount? Explain.

Make up your own number pattern and describe it.

✔ Checkpoint Describe the pattern.

1.	**2.**
3. 4, 8, 12, 16, 20, 24, ...	**4.** 35, 30, 25, 20, 15, 10, ...

Example 3 **Make a Prediction**

Sketch the next figure you expect in the pattern.

Solution

First notice how the shading changes. The color of the arrow changes back and forth between gray and black. The arrow in the next figure should be _____.

Also notice how the direction of the arrow changes. The arrow makes a _____ turn each time. In the next figure, the arrow should point _____.

Draw the next figure in the pattern.

Example 4 **Make a Prediction**

Write the next two numbers you expect in the pattern.

a. 5, 7, 9, 11, ...   b. −1, 3, −9, 27, ...

Solution

a. Notice that the numbers increase by ___ each time.

When you _____ 11, you get ___ . When you _____ , you get ___ .

Answer The next two numbers in the pattern are ___ and ___ .

b. Notice that the numbers switch from negative to positive in the pattern. This occurs when you multiply by a _____ number. Each number in the pattern is ____ times the previous number.

When you multiply 27 by ____ , you get ____ . When you multip _____ by ____ , you get ____ .

Answer The next two numbers in the pattern are ____ and ____

✓ *Checkpoint* Sketch the next two figures you expect in the pattern.

5.

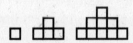

6.

Write the next two numbers you expect in the pattern.

7. −2, −5, −8, −11, ...	8. 4, 8, 12, 16, ...

1.2 Inductive Reasoning

Goal Use inductive reasoning to make conjectures.

VOCABULARY

Conjecture

Inductive reasoning

Counterexample

Example 1 *Make a Conjecture*

Complete the conjecture.

Conjecture: The sum of any two odd numbers is __?__.

Solution

Make sure you know the meaning of the conjecture.

A sum is _____.

The odd numbers are _____.

List some examples and look for a pattern.

$1 + 1 =$ __ $5 + 1 =$ __ $3 + 7 =$ ___

$3 + 13 =$ ___ $21 + 9 =$ ___ $101 + 235 =$ ___

Each sum is _____. So you can make a conjecture.

Answer The sum of any two odd numbers is _____.

Follow-Up

Which of the following reasoning stages were used in Example 1?

Look for a pattern   Make a conjecture   Verify a conjecture

Example 2   Make a Conjecture

Complete the conjecture.

Conjecture: The sum of the first n odd positive integers is __?__ .

Solution

The variable __ refers to the number of odd positive integers added together.

List some examples and look for a pattern.

For $n = 1$, the sum is $1 = 1 = \underline{}^2$

For $n = 2$, the sum is $1 + 3 = \underline{} = \underline{}^2$

For $n = 3$, the sum is $1 + 3 + 5 = \underline{} = \underline{}^2$

For $n = 4$, the sum is $1 + 3 + 5 + 7 = \underline{} = \underline{}^2$

For $n = 5$, the sum is $1 + 3 + 5 + 7 + 9 = \underline{} = \underline{}^2$

For any n, the sum is ___ .

Answer The sum of the first n odd positive integers is ___ .

Follow-Up Use the conjecture you made in Example 2 to find the sum of the first 8 odd positive integers.

For $n = 8$, the sum is ___, or ___.

Check your answer by adding the first 8 odd positive integers.

__ + __ + __ + __ + __ + __ + __ + __ = __

✔ **Checkpoint** Complete the conjecture based on the pattern in the examples.

1. The product of any two odd numbers is _____.

Examples: $1 \times 1 = 1$ $3 \times 5 = 15$ $3 \times 11 = 33$

$7 \times 9 = 63$ $11 \times 11 = 121$ $1 \times 15 = 15$

2. The product of the numbers $(n - 1)$ and $(n + 1)$ is _____.

Examples: $1 \cdot 3 = 2^2 - 1$ $3 \cdot 5 = 4^2 - 1$

$5 \cdot 7 = 6^2 - 1$ $7 \cdot 9 = 8^2 - 1$

$9 \cdot 11 = 10^2 - 1$ $11 \cdot 13 = 12^2 - 1$

Example 3   *Find a Counterexample*

Show the conjecture is false by finding a counterexample.

Conjecture: The sum of two numbers is always greater than the larger of the two numbers.

Solution

Here is a counterexample. Let the two numbers be 0 and 3. The sum is ___, which is not greater than ___, the larger of the two numbers.

Answer The conjecture is _____.

Find a different counterexample for Example 3.

Example 4   *Find a Counterexample*

Show the conjecture is false by finding a counterexample.

Conjecture: All shapes with four sides of the same length are squares.

Solution

Two counterexamples are shown at the right. These shapes have four sides of the same length, but they are not _____.

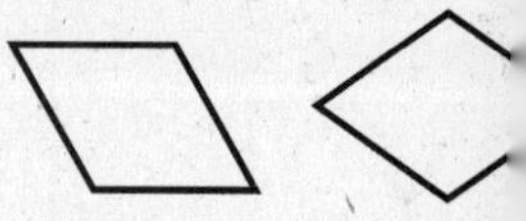

Answer The conjecture is _____.

✔ *Checkpoint* Show the conjecture is false by finding a counterexample.

3. If the product of two numbers is even, then the numbers must be even.

4. If a four-sided shape has two sides the same length, then it must be a rectangle.

Points, Lines, and Planes

Goal Use postulates and undefined terms.

VOCABULARY
_____

Undefined terms

_____

Point

_____

Line

_____

Plane

_____

Postulate

_____

Collinear points

_____

Coplanar points

_____

Coplanar lines

_____

Segment, Endpoints

_____

Ray

POSTULATE 1: TWO POINTS DETERMINE A LINE

Words Through any _____ points there is exactly one line.

Symbols Line *n* passes through points *P* and *Q*.

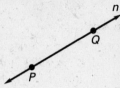

POSTULATE 2: THREE POINTS DETERMINE A PLANE

Words Through any _____ noncollinear points there is exactly one plane.

Symbols Plane *T* passes through points *A*, *B*, and *C*.

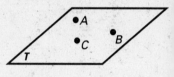

Example 1 *Name Points, Lines, and Planes*

Use the diagram at the right.

a. Name 3 points.

b. Name 2 lines.

c. Name 2 planes.

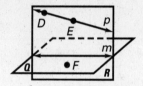

Solution

a. ___ , ___ , and ___   b. ___ and ___   c. ___ and ___

Example 2 *Name Collinear and Coplanar Points*

Use the diagram at the right.

a. Name three points that are collinear.

b. Name four points that are coplanar.

c. Name three points that are not collinear.

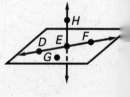

Solution

a. Points ___ , ___ , and ___ lie on the same line. So, they are collin[e]

b. Points ___ , ___ , ___ , and ___ lie on the same plane. So, they ar[e] coplanar.

c. Points ___ , ___ , and ___ do not lie on the same line. There are many correct answers.

✓ *Checkpoint* **Use the diagram shown.**

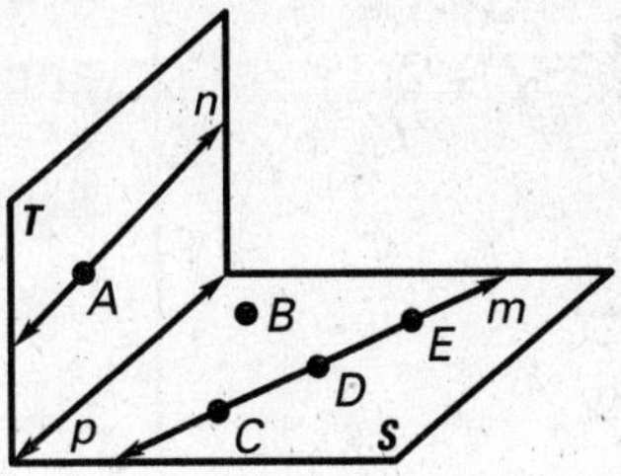

1. Name two lines.

_____

2. Name two planes.

3. Name three points that are collinear.

_____

4. Name three points that are not collinear.

_____

5. Name four points that are coplanar.

_____

6. Name two lines that are coplanar.

Follow-Up **Draw a diagram for each word.**

LINES, SEGMENTS, AND RAYS

Word	Symbol	Diagram
line	$\overleftrightarrow{AB}$ or $\overleftrightarrow{BA}$	
segment	$\overline{AB}$ or $\overline{BA}$	
ray	$\overrightarrow{AB}$	
	$\overrightarrow{BA}$	

Example 3 *Draw Lines, Segments, and Rays*

Draw three noncollinear points, *J*, *K*, and *L*. Then draw $\overleftrightarrow{JK}$, $\overline{KL}$, and $\overrightarrow{LJ}$.

Solution

Use the space at the right, and follow these steps.

1. Draw *J*, *K*, and *L* so that they are not collinear.
2. Draw $\overleftrightarrow{JK}$.
3. Draw $\overline{KL}$.
4. Draw $\overrightarrow{LJ}$.

Follow-Up Use your drawing in Example 3 to complete the table.

	Line, segment, ray?	How many arrowheads?	Name any endpoints.
$\overleftrightarrow{JK}$			
$\overline{KL}$			
$\overrightarrow{LJ}$			

✓ *Checkpoint* Use the four points shown.

7. Draw $\overleftrightarrow{AB}$ and $\overleftrightarrow{AC}$. Are the lines the same? Explain.

   A • B • C •

   _____

   • D

8. Draw $\overline{AC}$ and $\overline{BD}$. Are the segments the same? Explain.

   _____

9. Draw $\overrightarrow{CA}$ and $\overrightarrow{CB}$. Are the rays the same? Explain.

1.4 Sketching Intersections

Goal Sketch simple figures and their intersections.

VOCABULARY

Intersect

Intersection

POSTULATE 3: INTERSECTION OF TWO LINES

Words If two lines intersect, then their intersection is a _____.

Symbols Lines *s* and *t* intersect at

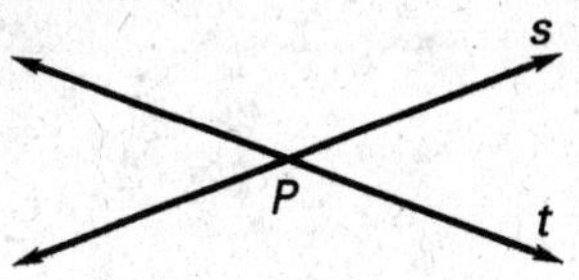

_____.

POSTULATE 4: INTERSECTION OF TWO PLANES

Words If two planes intersect, then their intersection is a _____.

Symbols Planes *M* and *N* intersect at _____.

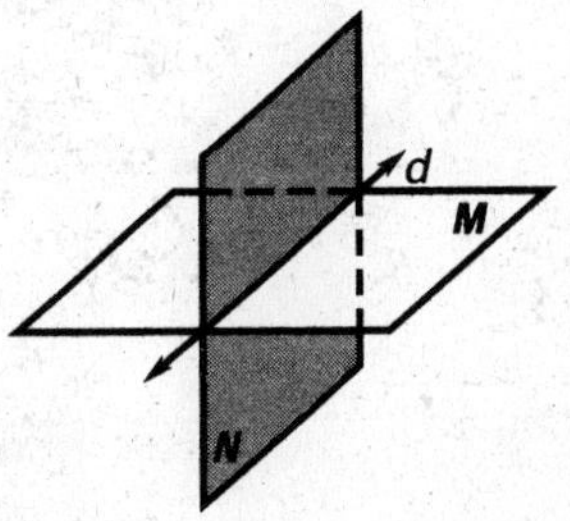

Follow-Up

Draw lines *k* and ℓ that intersect at point *Z*.	Draw lines *m* and *n* that do not intersect.

Example 1 *Name Intersections of Lines*

Use the diagram at the right.

a. Name the intersection of $\overleftrightarrow{AC}$ and $\overleftrightarrow{BE}$.

b. Name the intersection of $\overleftrightarrow{BE}$ and $\overleftrightarrow{DF}$.

c. Name the intersection of $\overleftrightarrow{AC}$ and $\overleftrightarrow{DF}$.

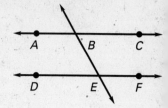

Solution

a. $\overleftrightarrow{AC}$ and $\overleftrightarrow{BE}$ intersect at _____.

b. $\overleftrightarrow{BE}$ and $\overleftrightarrow{DF}$ intersect at _____.

c. $\overleftrightarrow{AC}$ and $\overleftrightarrow{DF}$ do not appear to _____.

Follow-Up

In Example 1, do you think that $\overleftrightarrow{AC}$ and $\overleftrightarrow{DF}$ will ever intersect? Explain.

_____

In the figure at the right, do you think that lines *m* and *n* will ever intersect? Explain.

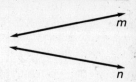

Example 2 *Name Intersections of Planes*

Use the diagram at the right.

a. Name the intersection of planes *S* and *R*.

b. Name the intersection of planes *R* and *T*.

c. Name the intersection of planes *T* and *S*.

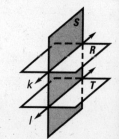

Solution

a. Planes *S* and *R* intersect at _____.

b. Planes *R* and *T* do not appear to _____.

c. Planes *T* and *S* intersect at _____.

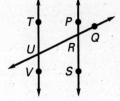

1. Name the intersection of $\overleftrightarrow{PS}$ and $\overleftrightarrow{QR}$.

_____

2. Name the intersection of $\overleftrightarrow{TV}$ and $\overleftrightarrow{QU}$.

_____

3. Name the intersection of $\overleftrightarrow{PS}$ and $\overleftrightarrow{UV}$.

Use the diagram shown.

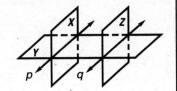

4. Name the intersection of planes X and Y.

_____

5. Name the intersection of planes Y and Z.

_____

6. Name the intersection of planes Z and X.

| Example 3 | *Sketch Intersections of Lines and Planes* |

Sketch a plane. Then sketch each of the following.

a. a line that is in the plane

b. a line that does not intersect the plane

c. a line that intersects the plane at a point

Solution

a.   **b.**   **c.**

Example 4   *Sketch Intersections of Planes*

Sketch two planes that intersect in a line.

Solution

1. Draw one plane as if you are looking straight at it. Shade the plane.

2. Draw a second plane that is horizontal. Shade this plane a different color.

3. Draw the line of intersection. Use dashed lines to show where one plane is hidden.

Follow-Up

Try to sketch two planes that intersect in exactly one point. Why is this impossible?

✔ *Checkpoint* Sketch the figure described.

7. Two lines that intersect a plane at the same point.

8. Two planes that intersect in a line.

9. Two planes that do not intersect.

1.5 Segments and Their Measures

Goal Measure segments. Add segment lengths.

VOCABULARY

Coordinate

Distance

Length

Between

Congruent segments

POSTULATE 5: SEGMENT ADDITION POSTULATE

Words and Symbols

If *B* is between *A* and *C*, then
AC = _____ + _____ .

If *AC* = _____ + _____ , then *B* is between *A* and *C*.

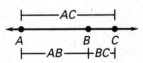

Follow-Up

What is the relationship between the two parts of Postulate 5?

Example 1   *Find the Distance Between Two Points*

Measure the lengths of $\overline{AC}$ and $\overline{BC}$ to the nearest millimeter.

Solution

Point *A* lines up with 0. Point *C* lines up with ___.

   $AC = |\_\_\_ - 0| = \_\_\_$ mm

Point *B* lines up with ___. Point *C* lines up with ___.

   $BC = |\_\_\_ - \_\_\_| = \_\_\_$ mm

✓ *Checkpoint* **Measure the length of the segment to the nearest $\dfrac{1}{8}$ inch.**

1. *A* ———————————————————— *B*

2. *C* ———————— *D*

Measure the length of the segment to the nearest millimeter.

3. *P* ———————— *Q*

4. *S* ————————————————

Example 2 — Find Distances on a Map

Use the map to find the distance from Athens to Albany.

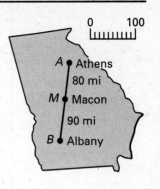

Solution

Because the three cities lie on a line, you can use the Segment Addition Postulate.

$AM =$ ___ miles $MB =$ ___ miles

$AB = AM + MB =$ ___ $+$ ___

$ =$ ___ miles

Answer The distance from Athens to Albany is _____.

Example 3 — Find a Distance by Subtracting

Use the diagram to find *EF*.

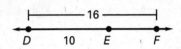

Solution

$DF =$ ___ $+$ ___   Use the Segment Addition Postulate.

___ $=$ ___ $+$ ___   Substitute values for *DF* and *DE*.

___ $= EF$ Solve for *EF*.

✓ **Checkpoint** Find the unmarked length.

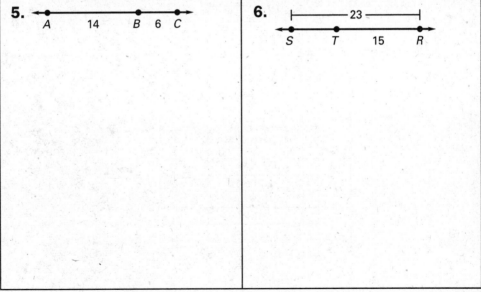

5.

6.

Example 4 **Decide Whether Segments are Congruent**

Are the segments shown in the coordinate plane congruent?

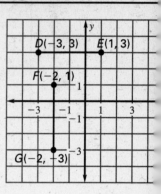

Solution

For a horizontal segment, subtract the x-coordinates.

$DE = |\_\_ - \_\_\_| = |\_\_| = \_\_$

For a vertical segment, subtract the y-coordinates.

$FG = |\_\_\_ - \_\_| = |\_\_\_| = \_\_$

Answer DE ___ FG, so $\overline{DE}$ ___ $\overline{FG}$.

✓ **Checkpoint** Plot the points in a coordinate plane. Then decide whether $\overline{AB}$ and $\overline{CD}$ are congruent.

7. $A(-2, 3), B(3, 3), C(-3, 4), D(-3, -1)$

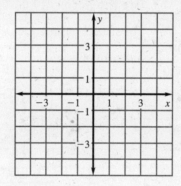

8. $A(0, 5), B(0, -1), C(4, 0), D(-1, 0)$

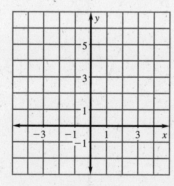

1.6 Angles and Their Measures

Goal Measure and classify angles. Add angle measures.

VOCABULARY

Angle, Sides, Vertex

Measure of an angle, degrees

Congruent angles

Acute angle

Right angle

Obtuse angle

Straight angle

Example 1   *Name Angles*

Name the angles in the figure.

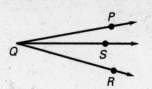

Solution

There are three different angles.

∠PQS or _____   ∠SQR or _____   ∠PQR or _____

Follow-Up

In Example 1, why should you *not* name any of the angles ∠Q?

✓ *Checkpoint* **Name the angles in the figure.**

1. 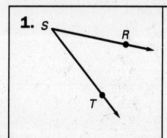	**2.** 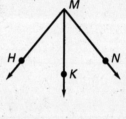	**3.** 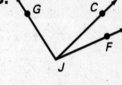

Example 2   *Measure Angles*

Use a protractor to approximate
the measure of ∠BAC.

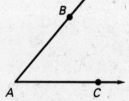

Solution

Put the center of the protractor over
the vertex point *A*.

Align the protractor with one side of
the angle.

The second side of the angle crosses the protractor at the 50°
mark. So, m∠BAC = _____.

Example 3   Classify Angles

Classify each angle.

a. $m\angle A = 130°$ **b.** $m\angle B = 90°$ **c.** $m\angle C = 45°$

Solution

a. $\angle A$ is _____ because its measure is greater than 90°.

b. $\angle B$ is _____ because its measure is 90°.

c. $\angle C$ is _____ because its measure is less than 90°.

Follow-Up Use your protractor to sketch each angle in Example 3.

$\angle A$	$\angle B$	$\angle C$

✔ ***Checkpoint*** Classify the angle.

4. $m\angle D = 17°$	**5.** $m\angle E = 180°$	**6.** $m\angle F = 173°$

POSTULATE 6: ANGLE ADDITION POSTULATE

Words If P is in the interior of $\angle RST$, then the measure of $\angle RST$ is the _____ of the measures of $\angle RSP$ and $\angle PST$.

Symbols If P is in the interior of $\angle RST$, then $m\angle RSP + m\angle PST =$ _____ .

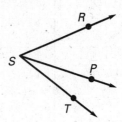

Follow-Up **Compare and contrast the Angle Addition Postulate with the Segment Addition Postulate in Lesson 1.5.**

How are they alike?

How are they different?

Example 4 **Add Angle Measures**

Find the measure of ∠*PTM*.

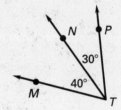

Solution

m∠*PTM* = _____ + _____   **Angle Addition Postulate**

m∠*PTM* = ____ + ____   **Substitute angle measures.**

m∠*PTM* = ____   **Add angle measures.**

Answer The measure of ∠*PTM* is ____ .

✔ ***Checkpoint*** **Find the measure of** ∠*ABC*.

7.	8.	9.
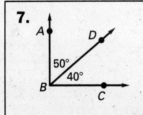	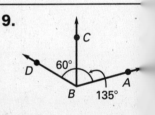	

Words to Review

Give an example of the vocabulary word.

Conjecture	Point, line, plane
Postulate	Collinear points
Coplanar points	Coplanar lines
Segment, endpoints	Ray

Intersect, Intersection	Coordinate
Distance	Length of a segment
Between	Congruent segments
Angle, Sides, Vertex	Measure of an angle, degrees

Congruent angles	Acute angle
Right angle	**Obtuse angle**
Straight angle	

Review your notes and Chapter 1 by using the Summary and Review on pages 42–45 of your textbook.

2.1 Segment Bisectors

Goal Bisect a segment. Find the coordinates of the midpoint of a segment.

VOCABULARY

Midpoint

Segment bisector

Bisect

Example 1 *Find Segment Lengths*

M is the midpoint of $\overline{AB}$. Find *AM* and *MB*.

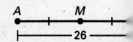

Solution

M is the midpoint of $\overline{AB}$, so *AM* is _____ of *AB*.

$$AM = \frac{1}{2} \cdot AB = \frac{1}{2} \cdot \underline{\quad} = \underline{\quad}$$

$$MB = AM = \underline{\quad}$$

Answer *AM* = ___ and *MB* = ___.

Example 2   *Find Segment Lengths*

P is the midpoint of $\overline{RS}$. Find *PS* and *RS*.

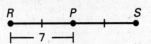

Solution

P is the midpoint of $\overline{RS}$, so *PS* = *RP* = __ .

You know that *RS* is twice *RP*.

   RS = __ · *RP* = __ · __ = __

Answer *PS* = __ and *RS* = __ .

Follow-Up

> How are Examples 1 and 2 different?

✔ *Checkpoint* **Complete the following exercises.**

1. Find *DE* and *EF*.	**2.** Find *NO* and *MO*.

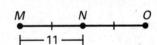

Example 3   *Use Algebra with Segment Lengths*

Line *l* is a segment bisector of $\overline{AB}$.
Find the value of *x*.

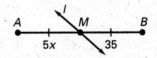

Solution

   M is the midpoint, so write an equation.   *AM* = *MB*

   Substitute values for *AM* and *MB*.   ___ = ___

   Solve for *x*.   *x* = __

THE MIDPOINT FORMULA

Words The coordinates of the midpoint of $\overline{AB}$ are the _____ of the x-coordinates and the y-coordinates of the endpoints.

Symbols The midpoint of the segment joining $A(x_1, y_1)$ and $B(x_2, y_2)$ is

$$M\left(\underline{\hspace{2cm}}, \underline{\hspace{2cm}}\right).$$

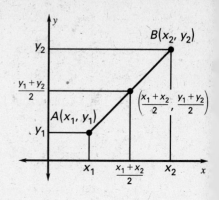

Example 4   *Use the Midpoint Formula*

Find the coordinates of the midpoint of $\overline{AB}$ for $A(1, 2)$ and $B(7, 4)$.

Solution

Plot A and B. Draw $\overline{AB}$. Then use the Midpoint Formula. Let $(x_1, y_1) = (1, 2)$ and $(x_2, y_2) = (7, 4)$.

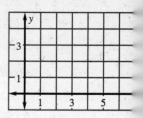

$$M = \left(\frac{x_1 + x_2}{2}, \frac{y_1 + y_2}{2}\right)$$

$$= \left(\underline{\hspace{1.5cm}}, \underline{\hspace{1.5cm}}\right)$$

$$= (\underline{\hspace{0.5cm}}, \underline{\hspace{0.5cm}})$$

✔ **Checkpoint** Sketch $\overline{PQ}$. Then find the coordinates of its midpoint.

---

3. $P(2, 5)$, $Q(4, 3)$

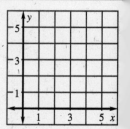

2.2 Angle Bisectors

Goal Bisect an angle.

VOCABULARY

Angle bisector

Example 1 *Find Angle Measures*

$\overrightarrow{BD}$ bisects $\angle ABC$, and $m\angle ABC = 110°$.
Find $m\angle ABD$ and $m\angle DBC$.

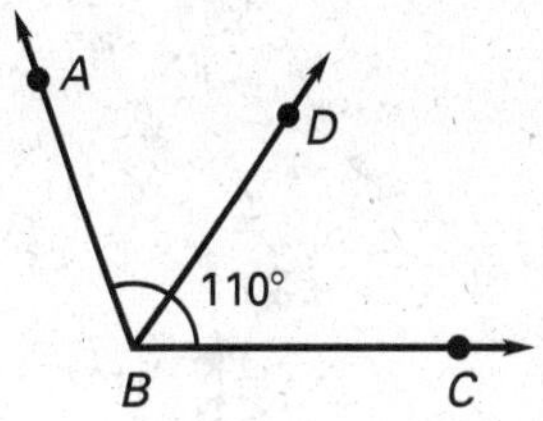

Solution

$\overrightarrow{BD}$ bisects $\angle ABC$, so $m\angle ABD$ is half of
$m\angle ABC$.

$m\angle ABD = \underline{\quad} \cdot m\angle ABC$

$\qquad = \underline{\quad} \cdot \underline{\quad}$

$\qquad = \underline{\quad}$

Answer $m\angle DBC = m\angle ABD = \underline{\quad}$

✓ **Checkpoint** $\overrightarrow{HK}$ bisects $\angle GHJ$. Find $m\angle GHK$ and $m\angle KHJ$.

1.	2.	3.

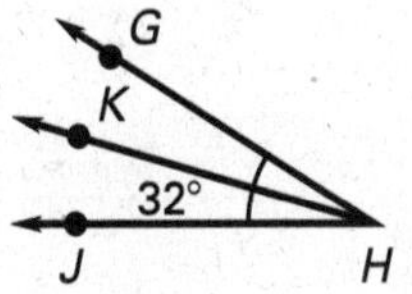

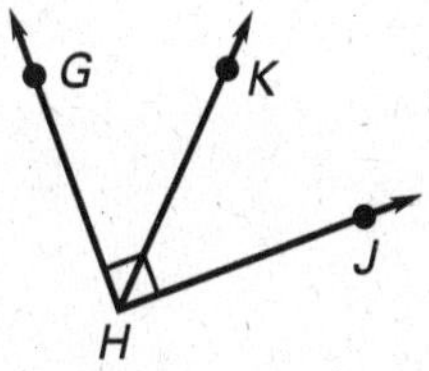

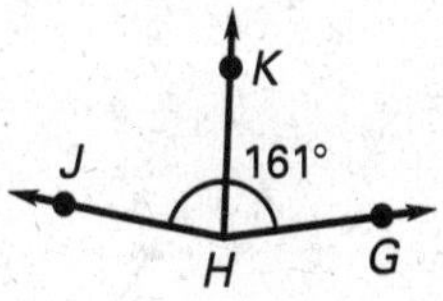

Example 2 **Angle Measures and Classification**

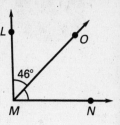

$\overrightarrow{MO}$ bisects $\angle LMN$, and $m\angle LMO = 46°$.

a. Find $m\angle OMN$ and $m\angle LMN$.

b. Determine whether $\angle LMN$ is *acute*, *right*, *obtuse*, or *straight*. Explain.

Solution

a. $\overrightarrow{MO}$ bisects $\angle LMN$, so $m\angle LMO = m\angle OMN$.

$m\angle OMN = m\angle LMO = $ ____

The measure of $\angle LMN$ is twice the measure of $\angle LMO$.

$m\angle LMN = $ __ $\cdot m\angle LMO = $ __ $\cdot$ ____ $= $ ____

b. $\angle LMN$ is _____ because its measure is between $90°$ and 180

✓ **Checkpoint** $\overrightarrow{QS}$ bisects $\angle PQR$. Find $m\angle SQP$ and $m\angle PQR$. The tell whether $\angle PQR$ is *acute*, *right*, *obtuse*, or *straight*.

4. 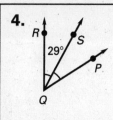	5. 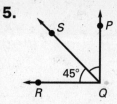	6. 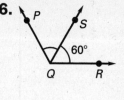

Example 3 **Use Algebra with Angle Measures**

$\overrightarrow{RQ}$ bisects $\angle PRS$. Find the value of x.

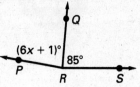

Solution

$m\angle PRQ = m\angle QRS$	$\overrightarrow{RQ}$ bisects $\angle PRS$.
$(\underline{\hspace{2cm}})° = \underline{\hspace{1cm}}$	Substitute the given angle measures.
$\underline{\hspace{3cm}} = \underline{\hspace{2cm}}$	Subtract __ from each side.
$\underline{\hspace{1cm}} = \underline{\hspace{1cm}}$	Simplify.
$\dfrac{\underline{\hspace{1cm}}}{\underline{\hspace{1cm}}} = \dfrac{\underline{\hspace{1cm}}}{\underline{\hspace{1cm}}}$	Divide each side by __.
$x = \underline{\hspace{1cm}}$	Simplify.

Follow-Up Check your answer for Example 3.

Substitute your value of x in the original equation to determine whether it is a solution.

✔ ***Checkpoint*** $\overrightarrow{BD}$ bisects $\angle ABC$. Find the value of x.

7.

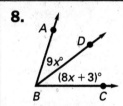

8.

Complementary and Supplementary Angles

Goal Find measures of complementary and supplementary angles.

VOCABULARY

Complementary angles

Complement

Supplementary angles

Supplement

Adjacent angles

Theorem

Follow-Up Think of a way to help you remember the meaning of each term.

Complementary angles

Supplementary angles

Example 1 — Identify Angles

State whether the angles are *complementary*, *supplementary*, or *neither*.

a.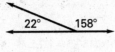

b.

c.

Solution

a. Because 22° + 158° = _____ , the angles are _____ .

b. Because 15° + 85° = _____ , the angles are _____ .

c. Because 55° + 35° = _____ , the angles are _____ .

Example 2 — Identify Adjacent Angles

State whether the numbered angles are *adjacent* or *nonadjacent*.

a.

b.

c.

Solution

a. Because the angles do not share a common vertex or side, ∠1 and ∠2 are _____ .

b. Because the angles share a common _____ and _____ , ∠3 and ∠4 are _____ .

c. Although ∠5 and ∠6 share a common _____ , they do not share a common _____ . Therefore, ∠5 and ∠6 are _____ .

Example 3   *Complements and Supplements*

a. ∠A is a complement of ∠C, and m∠A = 47°. Find m∠C.

b. ∠P is a supplement of ∠R, and m∠R = 36°. Find m∠P.

Solution

a. ∠A and ∠C are complements, so m∠A + m∠C = ____.

   ____ + m∠C = ____   **Substitute for m∠A.**

   m∠C = ____   **Solve for m∠C.**

b. ∠P and ∠R are supplements, so m∠P + m∠R = ____.

   m∠P + ____ = ____   **Substitute for m∠R.**

   m∠P = ____   **Solve for m∠P.**

✓ **Checkpoint** State whether the angles are *complementary, supplementary,* or *neither.*

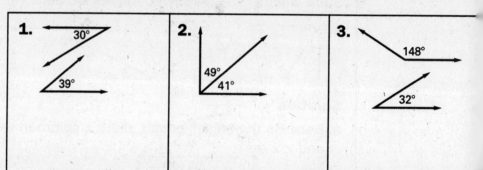

1. 30° 39°	2. 49° 41°	3. 148° 32°

4. ∠B is a complement of ∠D, and m∠D = 79°. Find m∠B.

5. ∠G is a supplement of ∠H, and m∠G = 115°. Find m∠H.

THEOREM 2.1: CONGRUENT COMPLEMENTS THEOREM

Words If two angles are complementary to the same angle, then they are _____.

Symbols If $m\angle 1 + m\angle 2 = 90°$ and $m\angle 2 + m\angle 3 = 90°$, then $\angle\_\_ \cong \angle\_\_$.

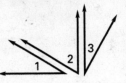

THEOREM 2.2: CONGRUENT SUPPLEMENTS THEOREM

Words If two angles are supplementary to the same angle, then they are _____.

Symbols If $m\angle 4 + m\angle 5 = 180°$ and $m\angle 5 + m\angle 6 = 180°$, then $\angle\_\_ \cong \angle\_\_$.

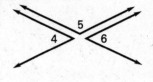

Example 4   Use a Theorem

$\angle 7$ and $\angle 8$ are supplementary, and $\angle 8$ and $\angle 9$ are supplementary. Name a pair of congruent angles. Explain your reasoning.

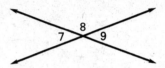

Solution

$\angle 7$ and $\angle 9$ are both _____ to $\angle 8$. So, from the Congruent _____ Theorem, it is true that $\angle\_\_ \cong \angle\_\_$.

✔ **Checkpoint** Complete the following exercise.

6. In the diagram, $m\angle 10 + m\angle 11 = 90°$, and $m\angle 11 + m\angle 12 = 90°$. Name a pair of congruent angles. Explain your reasoning.

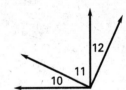

2.4 Vertical Angles

Goal Find the measures of angles formed by intersecting lines.

VOCABULARY

Vertical angles

Linear pair

Example 1   Vertical Angles and Linear Pairs

Determine whether the labeled angles are *vertical angles, a linear pair*, or *neither*.

a.   b.   c.

Solution

a. $\angle 1$ and $\angle 2$ are _____ because they are adjacent and their noncommon sides are on the same line.

b. $\angle 3$ and $\angle 4$ are _____.

c. $\angle 5$ and $\angle 6$ are _____ because they are not adjace and their sides are formed by two intersecting lines.

POSTULATE 7: LINEAR PAIR POSTULATE

Words If two angles form a linear pair, then they are supplementary.

Symbols $m\angle 1 + m\angle 2 = $ _____

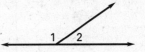

THEOREM 2.3: VERTICAL ANGLES THEOREM

Words Vertical angles are _____.

Symbols $\angle 1 \cong \angle 3$ and $\angle$ __ $\cong \angle$ __.

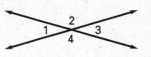

Example 2 **Use the Linear Pair Postulate**

Find the measure of $\angle RSU$.

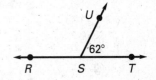

Solution

$\angle RSU$ and $\angle UST$ are _____. By the Linear Pair Postulate, they are _____.

$m\angle RSU = 180° - m\angle UST = $ ____ $-$ ____ $=$ ____

Example 3 **Use the Vertical Angles Theorem**

Find the measure of $\angle CED$.

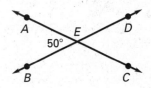

Solution

$\angle AEB$ and $\angle CED$ are _____ angles. By the Vertical Angles Theorem, _____ $\cong$ _____.

$m\angle CED = m\angle AEB = $ ____

Example 4   *Find Angle Measures*

Find $m\angle 1$, $m\angle 2$, and $m\angle 3$.

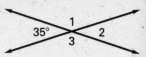

Solution

$m\angle 2 = \underline{\qquad}$ Use the Vertical Angles Theorem.

$m\angle 1 = 180° - \underline{\qquad} = \underline{\qquad}$ Use the Linear Pair Postulate.

$m\angle 3 = m\angle\underline{\quad} = \underline{\qquad}$ Use the Vertical Angles Theorem.

Example 5   *Use Algebra with Vertical Angles*

Find the value of y.

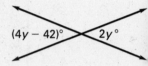

Solution

Because the two expressions are measures of vertical angles, you can write the following equation.

$(4y - 42)° = \underline{\qquad}$ Vertical Angles Theorem

$4y - 42 - \underline{\quad} = 2y - \underline{\quad}$ Subtract ____ from each side.

$\underline{\qquad} = \underline{\qquad}$ Simplify.

$\dfrac{\underline{\qquad}}{\underline{\qquad}} = \dfrac{\underline{\qquad}}{\underline{\qquad}}$ Divide each side by ____ .

$\underline{\quad} = y$ Simplify.

Follow-Up Check your answer for Example 5.

Substitute your value for y in the original equation to determine whether it is a solution.

✓ Checkpoint Find $m\angle 1$, $m\angle 2$, and $m\angle 3$.

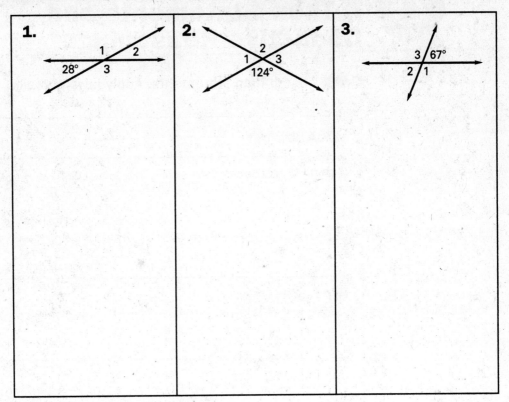

Find the value of the variable.

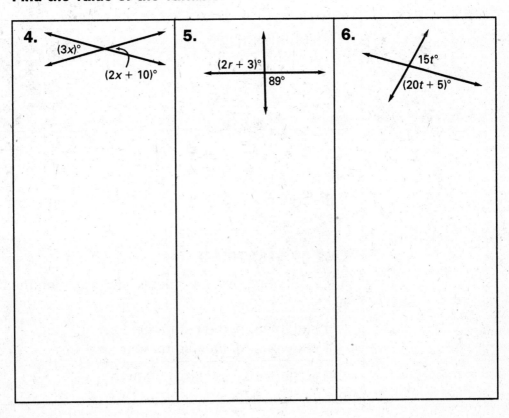

If-Then Statements and Deductive Reasoning

Goal Use if-then statements. Apply laws of logic.

VOCABULARY

If-then statement

Hypothesis

Conclusion

Deductive reasoning

LAW OF DETACHMENT

If the hypothesis of a true if-then statement is true, then the conclusion is _____.

LAW OF SYLLOGISM

If the following two statements are true, then the third statement is _____.

If statement *p*, then statement *q*.
If statement *q*, then statement *r*.

If statement __, then statement __.

Example 1 *Identify the Hypothesis and Conclusion*

Identify the hypothesis and conclusion of the if-then statement.

"If I pass the driving test, then I will get my driver's license."

Solution

Hypothesis: _____

Conclusion: _____

Example 2 *Write If-Then Statements*

Rewrite the statement as an if-then statement.

a. Every game on my computer is fun to play.

b. I will buy the CD if it costs less than $15.

Solution

a. If _____ , then _____ .

b. If _____ , then _____ .

Follow-Up

In a sentence that contains a hypothesis and a conclusion, is the conclusion always stated at the end of the sentence? Explain.

✔ *Checkpoint* Rewrite the statement as an if-then statement. Then identify the hypothesis and the conclusion.

1. An angle is obtuse if its measure is 170°.

Hypothesis:

Conclusion:

Example 3   *Use the Law of Detachment*

What can you conclude from the following true statements?

> If you wash the cotton T-shirt in hot water, then it will shrink.

> You wash the cotton T-shirt in hot water.

Solution

The hypothesis of a true if-then statement (the first statement) is true because of the second statement. By the Law of Detachment, the conclusion is also _____.

Answer You can conclude that _____.

✔ *Checkpoint* **What can you conclude from the given true statements?**

2. If x has a value of 7, then $2x - 3$ has a value of 11.

   The value of x is 7.

3. If you study at least 2 hours for the test, then you will pass the test.

   You study 3 hours for the test.

Example 4 **Judge the Correctness of an Argument**

Which argument about the statement below is correct?

If two angles are vertical angles, then they are congruent.

Argument 1:	**Argument 2:**
$\angle 1$ and $\angle 2$ are congruent. So, $\angle 1$ and $\angle 2$ are vertical angles.	$\angle 1$ and $\angle 2$ are vertical angles. So, $\angle 1$ and $\angle 2$ are congruent.

Solution

Argument ___ is correct. In this argument, the hypothesis (two angles are _____) is true, which implies that the conclusion (they are _____) is also true.

Example 5 **Use the Law of Syllogism**

Write the statement that follows from the true statements.

If the daily high temperature is 32°F or less, then the water in the pipe is frozen.

If the water in the pipe is frozen, then the pipe will break.

Solution

Use the Law of Syllogism.

If the daily high temperature is 32°F or less, then _____ _____.

✔ **Checkpoint** Write the statement that follows from the true statements.

4. If the ball is thrown at the window, it will hit the window.
   If the ball hits the window, then the window will break.

2.6 Properties of Equality and Congruence

Goal Use properties of equality and congruence.

REFLEXIVE PROPERTY

Equality

$AB = AB$

$m\angle A = $ _____

Congruence

$\overline{AB} \cong \overline{AB}$

$\angle A \cong $ ____

SYMMETRIC PROPERTY

Equality

If $AB = CD$, then $CD = AB$.

If $m\angle A = m\angle B$, then

_____.

Congruence

If $\overline{AB} \cong \overline{CD}$, and $\overline{CD} \cong \overline{AB}$.

If $\angle A \cong \angle B$, then _____.

TRANSITIVE PROPERTY

Equality

If $AB = CD$ and $CD = EF$,
then $AB = EF$.

If $m\angle A = m\angle B$ and
$m\angle B = m\angle C$, then

_____.

Congruence

If $\overline{AB} \cong \overline{CD}$ and $\overline{CD} \cong \overline{EF}$,
then $\overline{AB} \cong \overline{EF}$.

If $\angle A \cong \angle B$ and $\angle B \cong \angle C$,
then _____.

Example 1 *Properties of Equality and Congruence*

Name the property that the statement illustrates.

a. $DE = DE$

b. If $\angle P \cong \angle Q$ and $\angle Q \cong \angle R$, then $\angle P \cong \angle R$.

Solution

a. _____ Property of Equality

b. _____ Property of _____

✔ Checkpoint Name the property that the statement illustrates.

1. If $DF = FG$ and $FG = GH$, then $DF = GH$.

---

2. $\angle P \cong \angle P$

---

3. If $m\angle S = m\angle T$, then $m\angle T = m\angle S$.

Example 2   Use Properties of Equality

In the diagram, N is the midpoint of
$\overline{MP}$, and P is the midpoint of $\overline{NQ}$.
Show that $MN = PQ$.

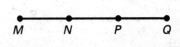

Solution

$MN = $ _____   Definition of midpoint

_____ $= PQ$ Definition of midpoint

$MN = PQ$ _____   Property of _____

Follow-Up

In Example 2, there is an explanation for each step in the
solution. In general, what can be used to explain steps in a
solution?

✔ *Checkpoint* **Complete the following exercise.**

4. ∠1 and ∠2 are vertical angles and
∠2 ≅ ∠3. Show that ∠1 ≅ ∠3.

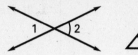

∠1 ≅ ∠2   _____ **Theorem**

∠2 ≅ ∠3   **Given**

∠1 ≅ ∠3   _____ **Property of Congruence**

ADDITION PROPERTY OF EQUALITY

Adding the same number to each side
of a true equation produces a true
equation.

$x - 3 = 7$
$x - 3 + 3 = 7$ __ __

SUBTRACTION PROPERTY OF EQUALITY

Subtracting the same number from
each side of a true equation produces
a true equation.

$y + 5 = 11$
$y + 5 - 5 = 11$ __ __

MULTIPLICATION PROPERTY OF EQUALITY

Multiplying each side of a true equation
by the same nonzero number produces
a true equation.

$\frac{1}{4}z = 6$

$\frac{1}{4}z \cdot 4 = 6$ __ __

DIVISION PROPERTY OF EQUALITY

Dividing each side of a true equation by
the same nonzero number produces a
true equation.

$8x = 16$
$8x \div 8 = 16$ __ __

SUBSTITUTION PROPERTY OF EQUALITY

Substituting a number for a variable in a
true equation produces a true equation.

$x = 7$
$2x + 4 = 2(\underline{\quad}) +$

Example 3   *Justify a Theorem*

∠1 and ∠2 are both supplementary to ∠3. Show that ∠1 ≅ ∠2.

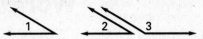

Solution

$m\angle 1 + m\angle 3 = $ _____	**Definition of supplementary angles**
$m\angle 2 + m\angle 3 = $ _____	**Definition of supplementary angles**
$m\angle 1 + m\angle 3 = m\angle 2 + m\angle 3$	_____ _____
_____ = _____	**Subtraction Property of Equality**
∠1 ≅ ∠2	_____ _____

✔ *Checkpoint* **Complete the following exercise.**

5. In the diagram, *M* is the midpoint of $\overline{AB}$. Show that $AB = 2 \cdot AM$.

A _____ M _____ B

$AM = MB$	**Definition of** _____
$AM + MB = AB$	_____ **Postulate**
$AM + AM = AB$	_____ **Property of Equality**
$2 \cdot AM = AB$	**Distributive property**

Words to Review

Give an example of the vocabulary word.

Midpoint	**Segment bisector**
Angle bisector	**Complementary angles, complements**
Supplementary angles, supplements	**Adjacent angles**
Theorem	**Vertical angles**

Linear pair	If-then statement
Hypothesis	Conclusion

Review your notes and Chapter 2 by using the Chapter Summary and Review on pages 95–97 of your textbook.

Relationships Between Lines

Goal Identify relationships between lines.

VOCABULARY

Parallel lines

Perpendicular lines

Skew lines

Parallel planes

Line perpendicular to a plane

Example 1 *Identify Parallel and Perpendicular Lines*

Determine whether the lines are *parallel, perpendicular,* or *neither.*

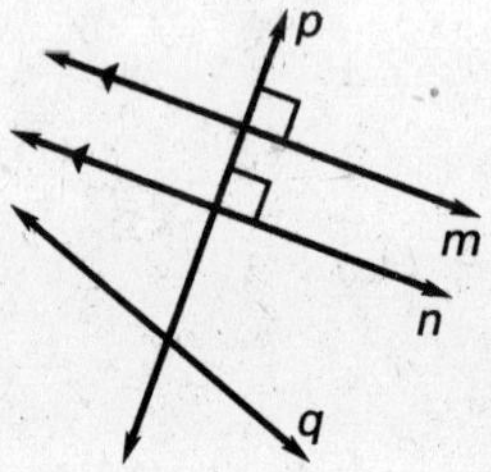

a. *n* and *m*

b. *p* and *q*

c. *n* and *p*

Solution

a. Lines *n* and *m* are _____ .

b. Lines *p* and *q* are _____ .

c. Lines *n* and *p* are _____ .

Follow-Up In Example 1, how do you know that the statement is true?

Lines *n* and *m* are parallel.

_____

Lines *n* and *p* are perpendicular.

_____

Lines *n* and *q* are not parallel.

_____

Lines *n* and *q* are not perpendicular.

Example 2   *Identify Skew Lines*

Determine whether the lines are skew.

a. *f* and *g*

b. *f* and *h*

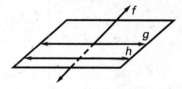

Solution

a. Lines *f* and *g* are not skew lines because _____.

b. Lines *f* and *h* are skew lines because _____

_____.

✓ *Checkpoint* Use the diagram shown.

1. Name a pair of parallel lines.

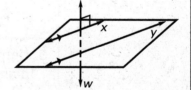

_____

2. Name a pair of perpendicular lines.

_____

3. Name a pair of skew lines.

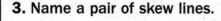

Example 3   *Identify Relationships in Space*

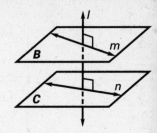

a. Name a plane that appears parallel to plane *B*.

b. Name a line that is perpendicular to plane *B*.

Solution

a. Plane ___ appears parallel to plane *B*.

b. Line ___ is perpendicular to plane *B*.

Follow-Up

In Example 3, is line *l* perpendicular to plane *C*? Explain.

In Example 3, is line *n* perpendicular to plane *C*? Explain.

✔ *Checkpoint* **Think of each segment in the diagram as part of a line.**

4. Name a line that is skew to $\overleftrightarrow{VW}$.

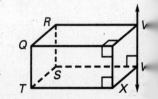

5. Name a plane that appears parallel to plane *VXW*.

6. Name a line that is perpendicular to plane *VXW*.

3.2 Theorems about Perpendicular Lines

Goal Use theorems about perpendicular lines.

THEOREM 3.1

Words All right angles are _____ .

Symbols If $m\angle A = 90°$ and $m\angle B = 90°$,
then $\angle A$ ___ $\angle B$.

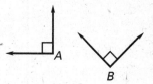

THEOREM 3.2

Words If two lines are perpendicular,
then they intersect to form _____ right angles.

Symbols If $n \perp m$, then $m\angle 1 =$ ____ ,
$m\angle 2 =$ ____ , $m\angle 3 =$ ____ , and $m\angle 4 =$ ____ .

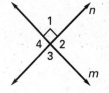

Follow-Up How do you know that each statement is true?

If two lines intersect to form a right angle, then they are
perpendicular lines.

If two lines are perpendicular, then they intersect to form four
right angles.

Example 1   *Perpendicular Lines and Reasoning*

In the diagram, $r \perp s$ and $r \perp t$. Decide whether enough information is given to conclude that the statement is true. Explain your reasoning.

a. $\angle 1 \cong \angle 5$

b. $\angle 4 \cong \angle 5$

c. $\angle 2 \cong \angle 3$

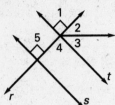

Solution

a. Enough information _____ given. $\angle 1$ and $\angle 5$ are both marked as _____ angles. By Theorem ____, $\angle 1$ ____ $\angle 5$.

b. Enough information _____ given. By Theorem 3.2, $\angle 4$ is a right angle because _____. $\angle 5$ is marked as a _____ angle. By Theorem ____, $\angle 4$ ____ $\angle 5$.

c. Enough information _____ given. $\angle 2$ and $\angle 3$ are not marked as congruent angles.

✓ **Checkpoint** In the diagram, $g \perp e$ and $g \perp f$. Decide whether enough information is given to conclude that the statement is true. Explain your reasoning.

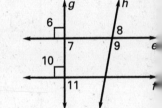

1. $\angle 6 \cong \angle 10$

2. $\angle 7 \cong \angle 10$

3. $\angle 6 \cong \angle 8$

4. $\angle 7 \cong \angle 11$

THEOREM 3.3

Words If two lines intersect to form adjacent congruent angles, then the lines are

_____.

Symbols If $\angle 1 \cong \angle 2$, then $\overleftrightarrow{AC}$ ___ $\overleftrightarrow{BD}$.

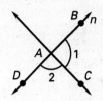

THEOREM 3.4

Words If two sides of adjacent acute angles are perpendicular, then the angles are

_____.

Symbols If $\overrightarrow{EF} \perp \overrightarrow{EH}$, then $m\angle 3 + m\angle 4 =$ ___.

Example 2   *Use Theorems about Perpendicular Lines*

In the helicopter at the right, are $\angle AXB$ and $\angle CXB$ right angles? Explain.

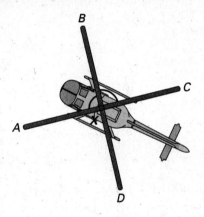

Solution

Use Theorem 3.3. $\overline{AC}$ and $\overline{BD}$ intersect to form _____,

so $\overline{AC}$ ___ $\overline{BD}$.

Use Theorem 3.2. $\overline{AC}$ and $\overline{BD}$ are _____, so $\angle AXB$ and $\angle CXB$ are _____.

Example 3 **Use Algebra with Perpendicular Lines**

In the diagram at the right, $\overrightarrow{EF} \perp \overrightarrow{EH}$ and $m\angle GEH = 30°$. Find the value of *y*.

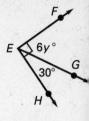

Solution

Use Theorem 3.4. ∠FEG and ∠GEH are adjacent acute angles, so they are _____.

$m\angle FEG + m\angle GEH = $ ____   ∠FEG and ∠GEH are

_____.

____ + ____ = ____   **Substitute angle measures.**

____ = ____   **Subtract ____ from each side.**

y = ____   **Divide each side by __.**

Follow-Up Check your answer in Example 3.

$m\angle FEG = 6y° = 6(10)° = $ ____ °

$m\angle FEG + m\angle GEH = $ ____ ° + ____ ° = ____ °

✓ *Checkpoint* Find the value of the variable. Explain.

5. ∠EFG ≅ ∠HFG

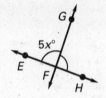

6. $\overrightarrow{AB} \perp \overrightarrow{AD}$

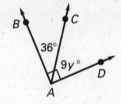

3.3 Angles Formed by Transversals

Goal Identify angles formed by transversals.

VOCABULARY

Transversal

Corresponding angles

Alternate interior angles

Alternate exterior angles

Same-side interior angles

Example 1   Describe Angles Formed by Transversals

Identify the relationship between the angles.

a. ∠1 and ∠2   **b.** ∠3 and ∠4   **c.** ∠5 and ∠6

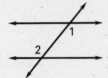
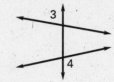
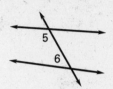

Solution

a. ∠1 and ∠2 are _____ angles.

b. ∠3 and ∠4 are _____ angles.

c. ∠5 and ∠6 are _____ angles.

Follow-Up On each diagram below, label the transversal *t*. Then label one pair of angles that fits the description.

∠1 and ∠6 are corresponding angles.	∠2 and ∠3 are alternate exterior angles.
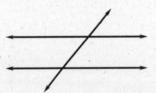	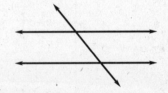
∠4 and ∠8 are alternate interior angles.	∠5 and ∠7 are same-side interior angles.
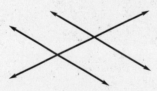	

Example 2   *Identify Angles Formed by Transversals*

List all pairs of angles that fit the description.

a. corresponding

b. alternate exterior

c. alternate interior

d. same-side interior

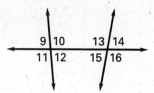

Solution

a. corresponding: $\angle 9$ and $\angle$___, $\angle 10$ and $\angle$___, $\angle$___ and $\angle$___, $\angle$___ and $\angle$___

b. alternate exterior: $\angle 9$ and $\angle$___, $\angle$___ and $\angle$___

c. alternate interior: $\angle 10$ and $\angle$___, $\angle$___ and $\angle$___

d. same-side interior: $\angle 10$ and $\angle$___, $\angle$___ and $\angle$___

Follow-Up

In Example 2, does a transversal intersect two parallel lines?

In the space at the right, draw two
lines intersected by a transversal *t*.

How many angles are formed?

Complete the table with the number of pairs of angles formed.

	Numbers of Pairs Formed
Corresponding angles	
Alternate exterior angles	
Alternate interior angles	
Same-side interior angles	

✔ _Checkpoint_ Describe the relationship between the angles in the diagram below.

1. ∠2 and ∠7

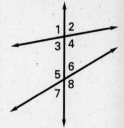

2. ∠3 and ∠5

3. ∠1 and ∠5

4. ∠4 and ∠5

5. ∠4 and ∠8

6. ∠4 and ∠6

3.4 Parallel Lines and Transversals

Goal Find the congruent angles formed when a transversal cuts parallel lines.

POSTULATE 8: CORRESPONDING ANGLES POSTULATE

Words If two parallel lines are cut by a transversal, then corresponding angles are _____ .

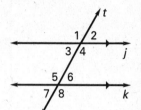

Symbols If $j \parallel k$, then the following are true.

$\angle 1 \cong \angle\underline{\quad}$ $\angle 2 \cong \angle\underline{\quad}$

$\angle 3 \cong \angle\underline{\quad}$ $\angle 4 \cong \angle\underline{\quad}$

Example 1   *Find Measures of Corresponding Angles*

Find the measure of the numbered angle.

a.
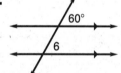

b.
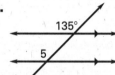

c.
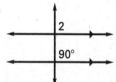

Solution

a. $m\angle 6 = $ ____ °   b. $m\angle 5 = $ ____ °   c. $m\angle 2 = $ ____ °

✔ **Checkpoint** Find the measure of the numbered angle.

1.	2.	3.
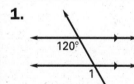	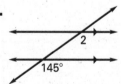	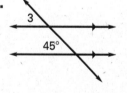

THEOREM 3.5: ALTERNATE INTERIOR ANGLES THEOREM

Words If two parallel lines are cut by a transversal, then alternate interior angles are _____.

Symbols If $j \parallel k$, then the following are true.

$$\angle 3 \cong \angle \_\_ \qquad \angle 4 \cong \angle \_\_$$

Example 2 *Find Measures of Alternate Interior Angles*

Find the measure of $\angle PQR$.

a. 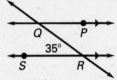   b. 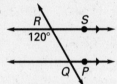   c.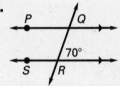

Solution

a. $m\angle PQR =$ ____°   b. $m\angle PQR =$ ____°   c. $m\angle PQR =$ ___°

✔ *Checkpoint* **Find the measure of the numbered angle.**

4.	5.	6.
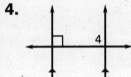	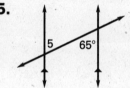	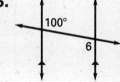

THEOREM 3.6: ALTERNATE EXTERIOR ANGLES THEOREM

Words If two parallel lines are cut by a
transversal, then alternate exterior angles
are _____ .

Symbols If $j \parallel k$, then the following are true.

$\angle 1 \cong \angle$____ $\angle 2 \cong \angle$____

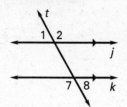

Example 3   *Find Measures of Alternate Exterior Angles*

Find the measures of $\angle 1$ and $\angle 2$.

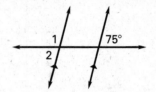

Solution

$m\angle 2 =$ ____ °   Alternate exterior angles are congruent.

$m\angle 1 + m\angle 2 =$ ____ ° $\angle 1$ and $\angle 2$ form a _____ .

$m\angle 1 +$ ____ ° = ____ °   Substitute ____° for $m\angle 2$.

$m\angle 1 =$ ____ °   Subtract ____° from each side and simplify.

Answer $m\angle 1 =$ ____ ° and $m\angle 2 =$ ____ °

✔ *Checkpoint* Find the measure of the numbered angle.

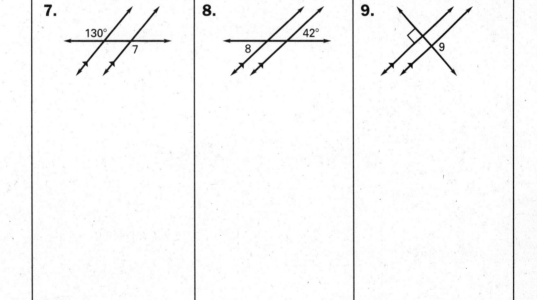

7.

8.

9.

THEOREM 3.7: SAME-SIDE INTERIOR ANGLES THEOREM

Words If two parallel lines are cut by a transversal, then same-side interior angles are _____.

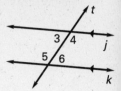

Symbols If $j \parallel k$, then the following are true.

$m\angle 3 + m\angle 5 =$ _____ ° $m\angle 4 + m\angle 6 =$ _____ °

Example 4   *Find Measures of Same-Side Interior Angles*

Find the measure of the numbered angle.

a.

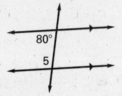

b.

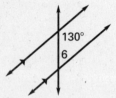

Solution

a. $m\angle 5 + 80° =$ _____ °
   $m\angle 5 =$ _____ °

b. $m\angle 6 + 130° =$ _____ °
   $m\angle 6 =$ _____ °

Example 5   *Use Algebra with Angle Relationships*

Find the value of x.

Solution

$(x + 15)° =$ _____ °   **Corresponding angles are congruent.**

$x =$ _____   **Subtract** _____ **from each side and simplify.**

✓ **Checkpoint** Find the value of x.

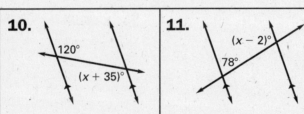

10.

120°
$(x + 35)°$

11.

$(x - 2)°$
78°

12.

$(2x + 10)°$

3.5 Showing Lines are Parallel

Goal Show that two lines are parallel.

VOCABULARY

Converse

Example 1 *Write the Converse of an If-Then Statement*

Statement: If two segments are congruent, then the two segments have the same length.

a. Write the converse of the true statement above.

b. Decide whether the converse is true.

Solution

a. Converse: _____

_____

b. The converse is a _____ statement.

✔ *Checkpoint* Write the converse of the true statement. Then decide whether the converse is true.

---

1. If two angles have the same measure, then the two angles are congruent.

_____

2. If ∠3 and ∠4 are complementary, then $m\angle 3 + m\angle 4 = 90°$.

_____

3. If ∠1 and ∠2 are right angles, then $\angle 1 \cong \angle 2$.

POSTULATE 9: CORRESPONDING ANGLES CONVERSE

Words If two lines are cut by a transversal so that corresponding angles are congruent, then the lines are _____.

Symbols If ∠1 ≅ ∠5, then r __ s.

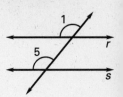

Example 2   Apply Corresponding Angles Converse

Is enough information given to conclude that $\overleftrightarrow{BD} \parallel \overleftrightarrow{EG}$? Explain.

a.
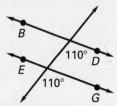

b.
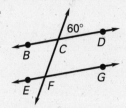

c.
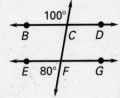

Solution

a. The 110° angles are corresponding and congruent. By the

_____, $\overleftrightarrow{BD} \parallel \overleftrightarrow{EG}$.

b. _____ information is given to conclude $\overleftrightarrow{BD} \parallel \overleftrightarrow{EG}$.

c. You can conclude that _____°. So, by the

_____, $\overleftrightarrow{BD} \parallel \overleftrightarrow{EG}$.

✔ **Checkpoint** Is enough information given to conclude that $\overleftrightarrow{RT} \parallel \overleftrightarrow{XZ}$?

4.	5.	6.
R X 85° 85° T Z	R S T 50° 130° X Y Z	R S T X Y Z

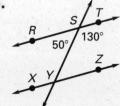
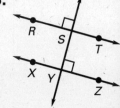

THEOREM 3.8: ALTERNATE INTERIOR ANGLES CONVERSE

Words If two lines are cut by a transversal so that alternate interior angles are congruent, then the lines are _____.

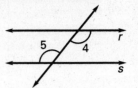

Symbols If $\angle 4 \cong \angle 5$, then r __ s.

THEOREM 3.9: ALTERNATE EXTERIOR ANGLES CONVERSE

Words If two lines are cut by a transversal so that alternate exterior angles are congruent, then the lines are _____.

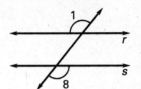

Symbols If $\angle 1 \cong \angle 8$, then r __ s.

Example 3   *Identify Parallel Lines*

Does the diagram give enough information to conclude that $m \parallel n$?

a.

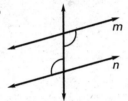

b.

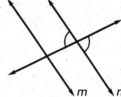

Solution

a. Yes. You can use _____ to conclude that $m \parallel n$.

b. No. Not enough information is given to conclude _____.

✔ *Checkpoint* **Complete the following exercise.**

7. Does the diagram give enough information to conclude that $c \parallel d$? Explain.

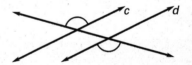

THEOREM 3.10: SAME-SIDE INTERIOR ANGLES CONVERSE

Words If two lines are cut by a transversal so that same-side interior angles are supplementary, then the lines are _____.

Symbols If $m\angle 3 + m\angle 5 = $ _____°, then $r \parallel s$.

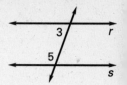

Follow-Up **Complete the statement.**

This lesson gives you four ways to show that two lines are _____.

Example 4 *Use Same-Side Interior Angles Converse*

Find the value of x so that $j \parallel k$.

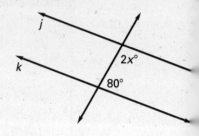

Solution

Lines j and k will be parallel if the marked angles are _____.

$$2x° + 80° = \underline{\quad}°$$ **Supplementary angles**

$$2x = \underline{\quad}$$ **Subtract ____ from each side.**

$$x = \underline{\quad}$$ **Divide each side by 2.**

✓ *Checkpoint* **Find the value of x so that $v \parallel w$.**

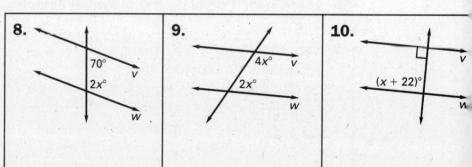

8.

9.

10.

3.6 Using Perpendicular and Parallel Lines

Goal Construct parallel and perpendicular lines. Use properties of parallel and perpendicular lines.

VOCABULARY

Construction

Example 1 *Construct Parallel Lines*

Construct a line that passes through point *P* and is parallel to line *l*.

Solution
Follow these steps.

1. Place the compass at point *P* and draw an arc that intersects line *l* twice. Label the intersections *A* and *B*.

2. Open your compass wider. Draw an arc with center *A*. Using the same radius, draw an arc with center *B*. Label the intersection of the arcs *Q*.

3. Use a straightedge to draw $\overleftrightarrow{PQ}$. $\overleftrightarrow{PQ}$ is _____ to line *l*.

4. Place the compass at point *P* and draw an arc that intersects $\overleftrightarrow{PQ}$ twice. Label the intersections *C* and *D*.

5. Open your compass wider. Draw an arc with center *C*. Using the same radius, draw an arc with center *D*. Label the intersection of the arcs *R*.

6. Use a straightedge to draw $\overleftrightarrow{PR}$.

Line *l* is _____ to $\overleftrightarrow{PR}$.

POSTULATE 10: PARALLEL POSTULATE

Words If there is a line and a point not on the line, then there is exactly one line through the point _____ to the given line.

Symbols If P is not on l, then there exists a line m through P such that _____ .

POSTULATE 11: PERPENDICULAR POSTULATE

Words If there is a line and a point not on the line, then there is exactly one line through the point _____ to the given line.

Symbols If P is not on l, then there exists a line m through P such that _____ .

THEOREM 3.11

Words If two lines are _____ to the same line, then they are parallel to each other.

Symbols If $q \parallel r$ and $r \parallel s$, then _____ .

THEOREM 3.12

Words In a plane, if two lines are _____ to the same line, then they are parallel to each other.

Symbols If $m \perp p$ and $n \perp p$, then _____ .

Follow-Up Does the construction of parallel lines shown in Example 1 use the following postulate or theorem?

Postulate 10	Postulate 11
Theorem 3.11	Theorem 3.12

Example 2 — Use Properties of Parallel Lines

In the diagram at the right, each rung on the ladder is parallel to the rung immediately below it, and the bottom rung is parallel to the ground. Explain why the top rung is parallel to the ground.

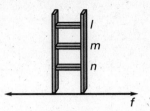

Solution

You are given that $l \parallel$ ___ and $m \parallel$ __. By Theorem 3.11, ____.
Since $l \parallel n$ and __ $\parallel f$, it follows that ____. So, the top rung is
parallel to the ground.

Example 3 — Use Properties of Parallel Lines

Find the value of x that makes $\overleftrightarrow{AB} \parallel \overleftrightarrow{CD}$.

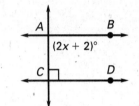

Solution

By Theorem 3.12, $\overleftrightarrow{AB}$ and $\overleftrightarrow{CD}$ will be parallel
if $\overleftrightarrow{AB}$ and $\overleftrightarrow{CD}$ are both _____ to
$\overleftrightarrow{AC}$. For this to be true, $\angle BAC$ must measure
___°.

$(2x + 2)° =$ ___° $m\angle BAC$ must be ___°.

$2x =$ ___   Subtract __ from each side.

$x =$ ___   Divide each side by __.

✔ **Checkpoint** Complete the following exercises.

1. Explain why $a \parallel c$. 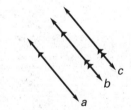	**2.** Find the value of x that makes $d \parallel e$. 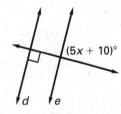

WAYS TO SHOW THAT TWO LINES ARE PARALLEL

Corresponding Angles Converse

Show that a pair of corresponding angles are _____.

Alternate Interior Angles Converse

Show that a pair of alternate interior angles are _____.

Alternate Exterior Angles Converse

Show that a pair of alternate exterior angles are _____.

Same-Side Interior Angles Converse

$m\angle 1 + m\angle 2 = 180°$

Show that a pair of same-side interior angles are _____.

Theorem 3.11

Show that both lines are are _____ to a third line.

Theorem 3.12

In a plane, show that both lines are _____ to a third line.

3.7 Translations

Goal Identify and use translations.

VOCABULARY

Translation

Image

Transformation

Example 1 | *Compare a Figure and Its Image*

Decide whether the gray figure is a translation of the black figure.

a.

b.

c.

Solution

a. This _____ a translation because the orientation _____ changed.

b. This _____ a translation because the orientation _____ changed. The image is a reflection of the original figure.

c. This _____ a translation because the orientation _____ changed. The original figure is rotated 90°.

Example 2 *Describe Translations*

Describe the translation of the segment.

Solution

To get from point P to point P', move
___ units to the right and ___ units down.
To get from point Q to point Q', move
___ units to the right and ___ units down.

So, every point on $\overline{PQ}$ moves _____ and _____.

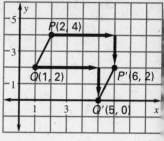

Example 3 *Use Coordinate Notation*

Describe the translation using
coordinate notation.

Solution

To get from point A to point A', move
___ units to the _____ and ___ units ___.

Use $(x, y) \rightarrow (x + a, y + b)$: $a = $ ____
and $b = $ ___.

Answer The translation can be described
using the notation $(x, y) \rightarrow$ _____.

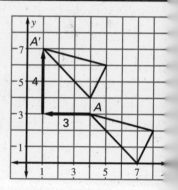

✔ *Checkpoint* **Complete the following exercises.**

1. Decide whether the
gray figure is a translation
of the black figure.

2. Describe the translation
using words and coordinate
notation.

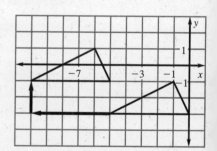

Example 4 *Draw Translated Figures*

Draw the triangle with vertices $A(-2, 5)$, $B(0, 7)$, and $C(3, 7)$.
Then draw the image of the triangle after the translation given
by $(x, y) \rightarrow (x + 2, y - 3)$.

Solution

Plot points A, B, and C. Draw $\triangle ABC$.

For the translation $(x, y) \rightarrow (x + 2, y - 3)$,
slide each point ___ units to the _____
and ___ units _____.

Plot points A', B', and C'. Draw $\triangle A'B'C'$.

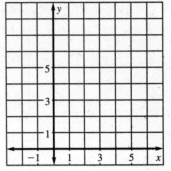

Follow-Up Use the translation in Example 4.

Complete the table below to show how the coordinates of
$\triangle A'B'C'$ relate to the notation $(x, y) \rightarrow (x + 2, y - 3)$.

$\triangle ABC$	$\triangle A'B'C'$
$A(-2, 5)$	$A'(-2 + 2, 5 - 3) = A'(0, 2)$
$B(0, 7)$	$B'(_____ , _____) = B'(\_\_, \_\_)$
$C(3, 7)$	$C'(_____ , _____) = C'(\_\_, \_\_)$

✓ **Checkpoint** Draw the image after the given translation.

3. $(x, y) \rightarrow (x + 3, y - 2)$

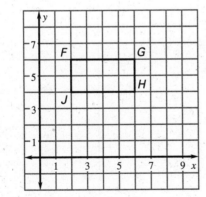

4. $(x, y) \rightarrow (x - 3, y + 4)$

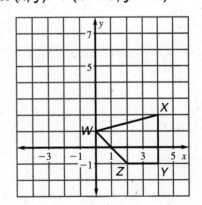

Words to Review

Give an example of the vocabulary word.

Parallel lines	Perpendicular lines
Skew lines	Parallel planes
Line perpendicular to a plane	Transversal
Corresponding angles	Alternate interior angles

Alternate exterior angles	Same-side interior angles
Converse	Translation, Image

Review your notes and Chapter 3 by using the Chapter Summary and Review on pages 160–163 of your textbook.

Goal Classify triangles by their sides and by their measures.

VOCABULARY

Triangle

Vertex

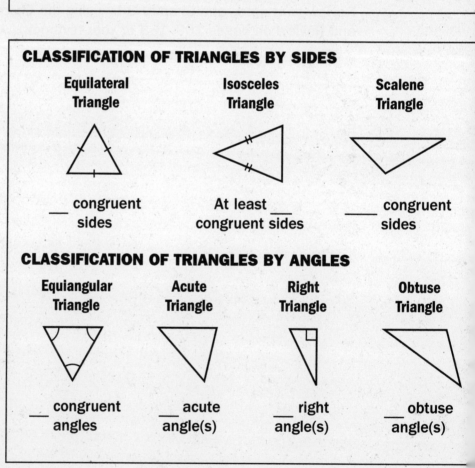

CLASSIFICATION OF TRIANGLES BY SIDES

Equilateral Triangle	Isosceles Triangle	Scalene Triangle
___ congruent sides	At least ___ congruent sides	___ congruent sides

CLASSIFICATION OF TRIANGLES BY ANGLES

Equiangular Triangle	Acute Triangle	Right Triangle	Obtuse Triangle
___ congruent angles	___ acute angle(s)	___ right angle(s)	___ obtuse angle(s)

Example 1   *Classify Triangles by Sides*

Classify the triangle by its sides.

a.   b.   c.

Solution

a. Because this triangle has ____ congruent sides, it is _____.

b. Because this triangle has ___ congruent sides, it is _____.

c. Because this triangle has ___ congruent sides, it is _____.

Example 2   *Classify Triangles by Angles and Sides*

Classify the triangle by its angles and by its sides.

a. 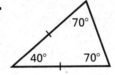   b.   c.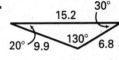

Solution

a. Because this triangle has 3 angles with measures less than 90°, it is _____. Because it has 2 congruent sides, it is _____. So, it is a(n) _____ triangle.

b. Because this triangle has a right angle, it is _____. Because it has no congruent sides, it is _____. So, it is a(n) _____ _____ triangle.

c. Because this triangle has one angle greater than 90°, it is _____. Because it has no congruent sides, it is _____. So, it is a(n) _____ triangle.

Follow-Up

Can a triangle be both acute and obtuse?

_____

Can a triangle be both equilateral and acute?

_____

Can a triangle be both scalene and isosceles?

✓ **Checkpoint** **Classify the triangle by its sides.**

1. 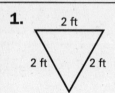	2. 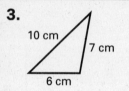	3. 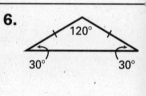

Classify the triangle by its angles and by its sides.

4.	5.	6. 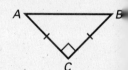

Example 3 *Identify the Parts of a Triangle*

Identify which side is opposite each angle.

Solution

$\overline{BC}$ is the side that is opposite _____ .

$\overline{AC}$ is the side that is opposite _____ .

$\overline{AB}$ is the side that is opposite _____ .

4.2 Angle Measures of Triangles

Goal Find angle measures in triangles.

VOCABULARY

Corollary

Interior angles

Exterior angles

THEOREM 4.1: TRIANGLE SUM THEOREM

Words The sum of the measures of the angles of a triangle is _____.

Symbols $m\angle A + m\angle B + m\angle C =$ _____.

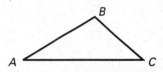

Example 1 *Find an Angle Measure*

Given $m\angle A = 35°$ and $m\angle B = 85°$, find $m\angle C$.

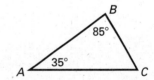

Solution

$m\angle A + m\angle B + m\angle C =$ _____	**Triangle Sum Theorem**
_____ + _____ + $m\angle C =$ _____	**Substitute for $m\angle A$ and $m\angle B$.**
_____ + $m\angle C =$ _____	**Simplify.**
$m\angle C =$ _____	**Subtract _____ from each side.**

Answer $\angle C$ has a measure of _____.

Follow-Up In Example 1, suppose a student found $m\angle C$ by calculating $180° - 35° - 85°$.

Does this method work? Explain.

Does this method use the Triangle Sum Theorem? Explain.

COROLLARY TO THE TRIANGLE SUM THEOREM

Words The acute angles of a right triangle are _____.

Symbols In $\triangle ABC$, if $m\angle C = 90°$, then $m\angle A + m\angle B =$ ____.

Example 2 *Find an Angle Measure*

△ABC and △BDC are right triangles. Suppose
m∠ABD = 35°. Find m∠DAB.

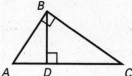

Solution

m∠DAB + m∠ABD = ____   **Corollary to the Triangle Sum Theorem.**

m∠DAB + ____ = ____   **Substitute for m∠ABD.**

m∠DAB = ____   **Subtract ____ from each side.**

THEOREM 4.2: EXTERIOR ANGLE THEOREM

Words The measure of an exterior angle of a
triangle is equal to the _____ of the measures
of the two nonadjacent _____ angles.

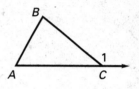

Symbols m∠1 = m∠A + _____

Example 3 *Find an Angle Measure*

Given m∠A = 58° and m∠C = 72°, find m∠1.

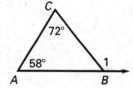

Solution

m∠1 = _____ + _____   **Exterior Angle Theorem**

m∠1 = ____ + ____   **Substitute.**

m∠1 = ____   **Simplify.**

Answer ∠1 has a measure of ____ .

✔ Checkpoint **Complete the following exercises.**

1. Find $m\angle A$.	**2.** Find $m\angle B$.	**3.** Find $m\angle C$.
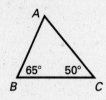	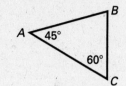	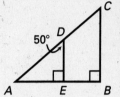
4. Find $m\angle 2$.	**5.** Find $m\angle 3$.	**6.** Find $m\angle 4$.
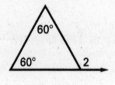	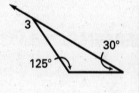	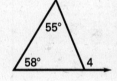

4.3 Isosceles and Equilateral Triangles

Goal Use properties of isosceles and equilateral triangles.

VOCABULARY

Legs of an isosceles triangle

Base of an isosceles triangle

Base angles of an isosceles triangle

THEOREM 4.3: BASE ANGLES THEOREM

Words If two sides of a triangle are congruent, then the angles opposite them are _____.

Symbols If $\overline{AB} \cong \overline{AC}$, then $\angle B \cong$ ____.

Example 1 *Use the Base Angles Theorem*

Find the measure of $\angle L$.

Solution

Angle L is a base of an isosceles triangle. From the Base Angles Theorem, $\angle L$ and ____ have the same measure.

Answer The measure of $\angle L$ is ____.

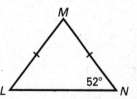

THEOREM 4.4: CONVERSE OF THE BASE ANGLES THEOREM

Words If two _____ of a triangle are congruent, then the _____ opposite them are congruent.

Symbols If $\angle B \cong \angle C$, then $\overline{AC} \cong$ ____.

Example 2   *Converse of the Base Angles Theorem*

Find the value of x.

Solution

By the Converse of the Base Angles Theorem, the legs have the same length.

$$TS = TP$$

$$x + \underline{\ \ } = \underline{\ \ \ }$$ Substitute for ____ and ____.

$$x = \underline{\ \ }$$ Subtract ___ from each side.

Answer The value of x is ___.

✔ *Checkpoint* Find the value of y.

1.

2.
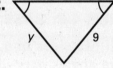

3.
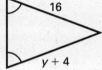

THEOREM 4.5: EQUILATERAL THEOREM

Words If a triangle is equilateral, then it is _____.

Symbols If $\overline{AB} \cong \overline{AC} \cong \overline{BC}$, then $\angle A \cong$ ____ $\cong$ ____.

THEOREM 4.6: EQUIANGULAR THEOREM

Words If a triangle is equiangular, then it is

_____.

Symbols If $\angle B \cong \angle C \cong \angle A$, then
$\overline{AB} \cong$ ____ $\cong$ ____.

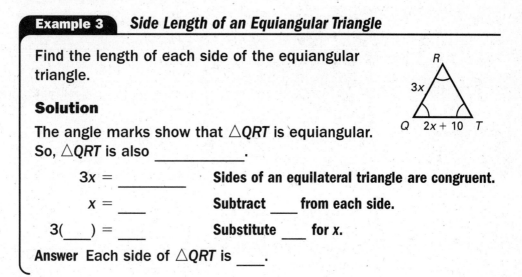

Example 3 *Side Length of an Equiangular Triangle*

Find the length of each side of the equiangular triangle.

Solution

The angle marks show that $\triangle QRT$ is equiangular. So, $\triangle QRT$ is also _____.

$3x =$ _____   Sides of an equilateral triangle are congruent.

$x =$ ___   Subtract ____ from each side.

$3(\_\_) =$ ___   Substitute ____ for x.

Answer Each side of $\triangle QRT$ is ___.

Follow-Up Compare Example 2 and Example 3.

How are they alike?

How are they different?

4.4 The Pythagorean Theorem and the Distance Formula

Goal Use the Pythagorean Theorem and the Distance Formula.

VOCABULARY

Legs of a right triangle

Hypotenuse

Distance Formula

THEOREM 4.7: THE PYTHAGOREAN THEOREM

Words In a right triangle, the square of the length of the _____ is equal to the sum of the squares of the lengths of the legs.

Symbols If $m\angle C = 90°$, then $c^2 =$ ___ + ___.

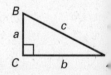

Example 1   *Find the Length of the Hypotenuse*

Find the length of the hypotenuse.

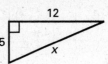

Solution

Use the Pythagorean Theorem to write an
equation of the form (hypotenuse)^2 = (leg)^2 + (leg)^2.

$x^2 = (\_\_)^2 + (\_\_)^2$ **Substitute.**

$x^2 = \_\_ + \_\_\_$ **Multiply.**

$x^2 = \_\_\_$ **Add.**

$\sqrt{x^2} = \_\_\_\_\_$ **Find the positive square root.**

$x = \_\_$ **Solve for x.**

Answer The length of the hypotenuse is ___.

Example 2   *Find the Length of a Leg*

Find the unknown side length.

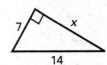

Solution

Use the Pythagorean Theorem to write an equation
of the form (hypotenuse)^2 = (leg)^2 + (leg)^2.

$(\_\_)^2 = (\_\_)^2 + (x)^2$ **Substitute.**

$\_\_\_\_ = \_\_ + x^2$ **Multiply.**

$\_\_\_\_ = x^2$ **Subtract ____ from each side.**

$\_\_\_\_\_ = \sqrt{x^2}$ **Find the positive square root.**

$\_\_\_\_\_ \approx x$ **Approximate with a calculator.**

Answer The side length is about _____ units.

1.

6   10

x

2.   15

17   x

3.

7   8

x

THE DISTANCE FORMULA

If $A(x_1, y_1)$ and $B(x_2, y_2)$ are points in a coordinate plane, then the distance between A and B is

$$AB = \sqrt{(\underline{})^2 + (\underline{})^2}.$$

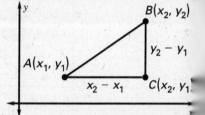

Example 3 **Use the Distance Formula**

Find the distance between D(1, 2) and E(3, −2).

Plot points D and E in a coordinate plane. Let $D(1, 2)$ be (x_1, y_1), so $x_1 = $ __ and $y_1 = $ __. Let $E(3, -2)$ be (x_2, y_2), so $x_2 = $ __ and $y_2 = $ ___.

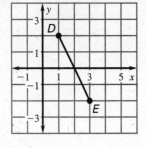

$DE = $ _____   **Distance Formula**

$= $ _____   **Substitute.**

$= $ _____   **Simplify.**

$= $ _____   **Add.**

$\approx $ _____   **Approximate with a calculator.**

Answer The distance between D and E is about ____ units.

Follow-Up

Can Example 3 be done using the Pythagorean Theorem rather than the Distance Formula? Explain.

✔ Checkpoint Find the distance between the points.

4.

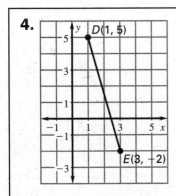

4.5 The Converse of the Pythagorean Theorem

Goal Use the converse of the Pythagorean Theorem. Use side lengths to classify triangles.

THEOREM 4.8: CONVERSE OF THE PYTHAGOREAN THEOREM

Words If the square of the length of the longest side of a triangle is equal to the sum of the squares of the lengths of the other two sides, then the triangle is a _____ triangle.

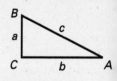

Symbols If $c^2 = a^2 + b^2$, then $\triangle ABC$ is a _____ triangle.

Example 1   *Verify a Right Triangle*

Is $\triangle ABC$ a right triangle?

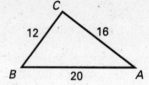

Solution

Let c represent the length of the longest side of the triangle. Check to see whether the side lengths satisfy the equation $c^2 = a^2 + b^2$.

$$c^2 \overset{?}{=} a^2 + b^2 \qquad \text{Compare } c^2 \text{ with } a^2 + b^2.$$

$$(\underline{})^2 \overset{?}{=} (\underline{})^2 + (\underline{})^2 \qquad \text{Substitute values for } a, b, \text{ and } c.$$

$$\underline{} \overset{?}{=} \underline{} + \underline{} \qquad \text{Multiply.}$$

$$\underline{} = \underline{} \qquad \text{Simplify.}$$

Answer It is _____ that $c^2 = a^2 + b^2$. So, $\triangle ABC$ _____ a right triangle.

Follow-Up

In Example 1, how do you know which side lengths to use for *a*, *b*, and *c*?

✔ *Checkpoint* **Is the triangle a right triangle? Explain your reasoning.**

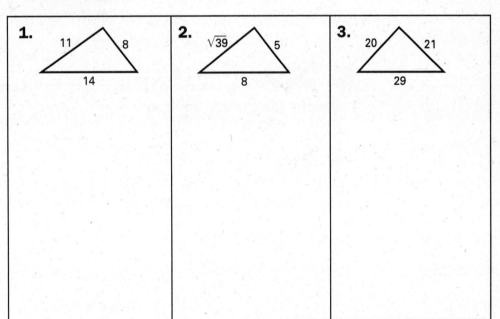

1. 11, 8, 14

2. √39, 5, 8

3. 20, 21, 29

CLASSIFYING TRIANGLES

In △*ABC* with the longest side *c*:

If $c^2 < a^2 + b^2$, then △*ABC* is _____.

If $c^2 = a^2 + b^2$, then △*ABC* is _____.

If $c^2 > a^2 + b^2$, then △*ABC* is _____.

Example 2   Acute Triangles

Show that the triangle is an acute triangle.

Solution

Compare the side lengths.

$$c^2 \stackrel{?}{=} a^2 + b^2$$ Compare c^2 with $a^2 + b^2$.

$$(\underline{})^2 \stackrel{?}{=} (\underline{})^2 + (\underline{})^2$$ Substitute for a, b, and c.

$$\underline{} \stackrel{?}{=} \underline{} + \underline{}$$ Multiply.

$$\underline{} \underline{} \underline{}$$ Simplify.

Answer Because $c^2 \underline{} a^2 + b^2$, the triangle is _____.

Example 3   Classify Triangles

Classify the triangle as *acute*, *right*, or *obtuse*.

Solution

Compare the square of the length of the longest side with the sum of the squares of the lengths of the two shorter sides.

$$c^2 \stackrel{?}{=} a^2 + b^2$$ Compare c^2 with $a^2 + b^2$.

$$(\underline{})^2 \stackrel{?}{=} (\underline{})^2 + (\underline{})^2$$ Substitute for a, b, and c.

$$\underline{} \stackrel{?}{=} \underline{} + \underline{}$$ Multiply.

$$\underline{} \underline{} \underline{}$$ Simplify.

Answer Because $c^2 \underline{} a^2 + b^2$, the triangle is _____.

Checkpoint Classify the triangle as *acute*, *right*, or *obtuse*. Explain.

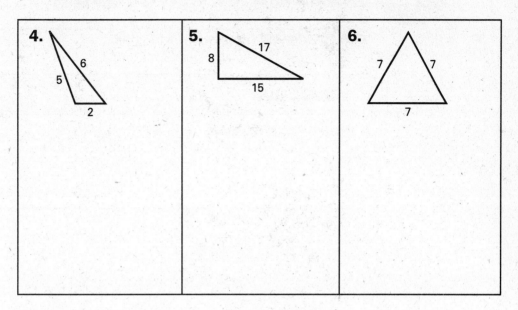

4.	**5.**	**6.**
6 5 2	17 8 15	7 7 7

Use the side lengths to classify the triangle as *acute*, *right*, or *obtuse*.

7. 7, 24, 24	**8.** 7, 24, 25	**9.** 7, 24, 26

4.6 Medians of a Triangle

Goal Identify medians in triangles.

VOCABULARY

Median of a triangle

_____

Centroid

THEOREM 4.9: INTERSECTION OF MEDIANS OF A TRIANGLE

Words The medians of a triangle intersect at a point that is _____ of the distance from each vertex to the _____ of the opposite side.

Symbols If P is the centroid of $\triangle ABC$, then

$$AP = \frac{2}{3}\underline{\quad}, \quad BP = \frac{2}{3}\underline{\quad}, \quad \text{and } CP = \frac{2}{3}\underline{\quad}.$$

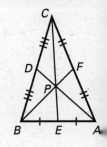

Example 1 *Draw a Median*

In $\triangle STR$, draw a median from S to its opposite side.

Solution

The side opposite $\angle S$ is ____.

Find the midpoint of ____, and label it P. Then draw a segment from point S to point P. $\overline{SP}$ is a median of $\triangle STR$.

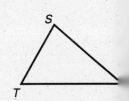

Example 2 *Use the Centroid of a Triangle*

E is the centroid of $\triangle ABC$ and *DA* = 27. Find *EA* and *DE*.

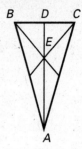

Solution

Using Theorem 4.9, you know that

$$EA = \frac{2}{3}DA = \frac{2}{3}(\underline{\quad}) = \underline{\quad}.$$

Use the Segment Addition Postulate to find *DE*.

$\underline{\quad}$ = DE + $\underline{\quad}$	**Segment Addition Postulate**	
$\underline{\quad}$ = DE + $\underline{\quad}$	**Substitute.**	
$\underline{\quad}$ = DE	**Subtract** $\underline{\quad}$ **from each side.**	

Answer $\overline{EA}$ has a length of $\underline{\quad}$ and $\overline{DE}$ has a length of $\underline{\quad}$.

Follow-Up In Example 2, use your answer to show that the following relationships are true.

$ED = \frac{1}{3}AD$	$AE = 2 \cdot ED$	$AD = ED + AE$

Example 3 *Use the Centroid of a Triangle*

P is the centroid of $\triangle QRS$ and *RP* = 10.
Find *RT*.

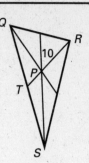

Solution

$RP = \dfrac{2}{3}RT$ Use Theorem 4.9.

$\underline{\hphantom{RP}} = \dfrac{2}{3}RT$ Substitute.

$\underline{\hphantom{RP}} = RT$ Multiply each side by $\underline{\hphantom{RP}}$.

Answer The median $\overline{RT}$ has a length of ____.

✓ *Checkpoint* **The centroid of the triangle is shown. Find the indicated lengths.**

1. Find *BE* and *ED*, given *BD* = 24.	**2.** Find *IG* and *JG*, given *IJ* = 4.	**3.** Find *ON* and *NL*, given *OL* = 20.
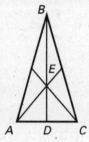	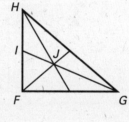	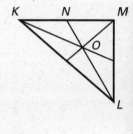

4.7 Triangle Inequalities

Goal Use triangle measurements to decide which side is longest and which angle is largest.

THEOREM 4.10

Words If one side of a triangle is longer than another side, then the angle opposite the longer side is _____ than the angle opposite the shorter side.

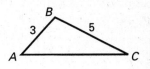

Symbols If $BC > AB$, then $m\angle A$ ___ $m\angle C$.

THEOREM 4.11

Words If one angle of a triangle is larger than another angle, then the side opposite the larger angle is _____ than the side opposite the smaller angle.

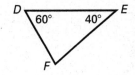

Symbols If $m\angle D > m\angle E$, then EF ___ DF.

Example 1 *Order Angle Measures*

Name the angles from largest to smallest.

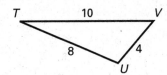

Solution

TV ___ TU, so $m\angle U$ ___ $m\angle V$.

TU ___ UV, so $m\angle V$ ___ $m\angle T$.

Answer The order of the angles from largest to smallest is _____, _____, _____.

Example 2   *Order Side Lengths*

Name the sides from longest to shortest.

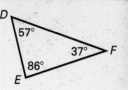

Solution

$m\angle E$ ___ $m\angle D$, so *DF* ___ *FE*.

$m\angle D$ ___ $m\angle F$, so *FE* ___ *DE*.

Answer The order of the sides from longest to shortest is ____,

____, ____.

Follow-Up

Which theorem is used in Example 1?

_____

Which theorem is used in Example 2?

✔ *Checkpoint* Name the angles from largest to smallest.

1.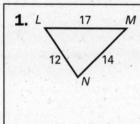

2.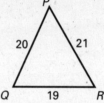

3.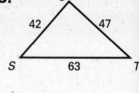

Name the sides from longest to shortest.

4.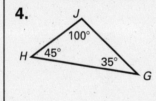

5.

6.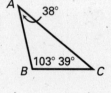

THEOREM 4.12: TRIANGLE INEQUALITY

Words The sum of the lengths of any two sides of a triangle is
_____ than the length of the third side.

Symbols

$CA + AB$ ___ BC

$AB + BC$ ___ CA

$BC + CA$ ___ AB

Example 3 *Use the Triangle Inequality*

Can the side lengths form a triangle? Explain.

a. 3, 5, 9   **b.** 3, 5, 8   **c.** 3, 5, 7

Solution

a.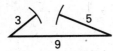

These lengths
do not form a
triangle, because
3 + 5 ___ 9.

b.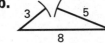

These lengths
do not form a
triangle, because
3 + 5 ___ 8.

c.

These lengths
do form a
triangle, because
3 + 5 ___ 7,
3 + 7 ___ 5, and
5 + 7 ___ 3.

✔ *Checkpoint* Can the side lengths form a triangle? Explain.

7. 5, 7, 13	**8.** 6, 9, 12	**9.** 10, 15, 25

Words to Review

Give an example of the vocabulary word.

Triangle, vertex	Equilateral triangle
Isosceles triangle	Scalene triangle
Equiangular triangle	Acute triangle
Right triangle	Obtuse triangle

Interior angle, exterior angle	Legs, base, base angles of an isosceles triangle
Legs, hypotenuse of a right triangle	Median of a triangle
Centroid	

Review your notes and Chapter 4 by using the Chapter Summary and Review on pages 219–223 of your textbook.

5.1 Congruence and Triangles

Goal Identify congruent triangles and corresponding parts.

VOCABULARY

Corresponding parts

Congruent

Example 1 *List Corresponding Parts*

Given that $\triangle JKL \cong \triangle SRT$, list all corresponding congruent parts.

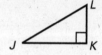

Solution

The order of the letters in the names of the triangles shows which parts correspond.

Corresponding Angles	Corresponding Sides
$\triangle JKL \cong \triangle SRT$ so $\angle J \cong \angle S$.	$\triangle JKL \cong \triangle SRT$ so $\overline{JK} \cong \overline{SR}$.
$\triangle JKL \cong \triangle SRT$ so $\angle K \cong \angle \underline{\quad}$.	$\triangle JKL \cong \triangle SRT$ so $\overline{KL} \cong \underline{\quad}$.
$\triangle JKL \cong \triangle SRT$ so $\angle \underline{\quad} \cong \angle \underline{\quad}$.	$\triangle JKL \cong \triangle SRT$ so $\underline{\quad} \cong \underline{\quad}$.

✔ *Checkpoint* Complete the following exercise.

---

1. Given $\triangle STU \cong \triangle YXZ$, list all corresponding congruent parts.

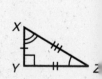

Example 2   *Write a Congruence Statement*

The two triangles at the right
are congruent.

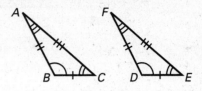

a. Identify all corresponding parts.

b. Write a congruence statement.

Solution

a. Congruent angles: $\angle A \cong \angle\underline{\quad}$, $\angle B \cong \angle\underline{\quad}$, $\angle C \cong \angle\underline{\quad}$

Congruent sides: $\overline{AB} \cong \underline{\quad}$, $\overline{BC} \cong \underline{\quad}$, $\overline{AC} \cong \underline{\quad}$

b. List the letters in the triangle names so that the corresponding
angles match. Using the order from part (a), one possible
congruence statement is $\triangle ABC \cong \triangle\underline{\quad}$.

Follow-Up

Write four different congruence statements for the triangles in
Example 2.

Example 3   *Use Properties of Congruent Triangles*

In the figure, $\triangle PQR \cong \triangle XYZ$.

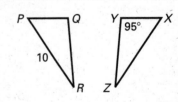

a. Find the length of $\overline{XZ}$.

b. Find $m\angle Q$.

Solution

a. Since $\overline{XZ} \cong \overline{PR}$, then $XZ = PR = \underline{\quad}$.

b. Since $\angle Q \cong \angle\underline{\quad}$, then $m\angle Q = m\angle\underline{\quad} = \underline{\quad}°$.

2. Given △*ABC* ≅ △*DEF*, find the length of $\overline{DF}$ and *m*∠*B*.

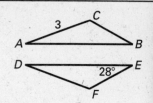

3. Use the triangles shown. Which congruence statement is correct? Why?

    A. △*JKL* ≅ △*MNP*

    B. △*JKL* ≅ △*NMP*

    C. △*JKL* ≅ △*PMN*

Example 4 *Decide Whether Triangles are Congruent*

Use the two triangles at the right.

a. Identify all pairs of corresponding congruent parts.

b. Determine if the triangles are congruent. If they are congruent, write a congruence statement.

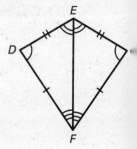

Solution

a. Angles: ∠*D* ≅ ∠___ , ∠*DEF* ≅ ∠_____ , ∠*DFE* ≅ ∠_____

    Sides: $\overline{EF}$ ≅ $\overline{EF}$, $\overline{DE}$ ≅ _____ , $\overline{DF}$ ≅ _____

b. All three sets of corresponding angles are congruent, and all three sets of corresponding sides are congruent, so the two triangles are _____ : △*DEF* ≅ △_____ .

Follow-Up

Name the property that tells you $\overline{EF}$ ≅ $\overline{EF}$ in Example 4.

Example 5   *Determine Whether Triangles are Congruent*

In the diagram at the right, $\overline{HG} \parallel \overline{LK}$.
Determine whether the triangles are
congruent. If they are, write a
congruence statement.

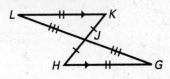

Solution

Find three pairs of corresponding angles that are congruent.

1. $\angle HJG \cong \angle KJL$ because _____.

2. As in the given figure, draw $\overline{HG} \parallel \overline{LK}$ cut
by transversal $\overline{KH}$. $\angle GHK \cong \angle LKH$ by the

_____.

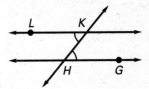

3. As in the given figure, draw $\overline{HG} \parallel \overline{LK}$ cut
by transversal $\overline{LG}$. $\angle HGL \cong \angle KLG$ by the

_____.

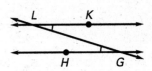

Find three pairs of corresponding sides that
are congruent.

$\overline{JG} \cong$ ____, $\overline{HJ} \cong$ ____, and $\overline{HG} \cong$ ____.

The triangles are congruent: $\triangle HJG \cong \triangle$_____.

✔ *Checkpoint* **Complete the following exercise.**

4. In the figure, $\overline{XY} \parallel \overline{WZ}$. Determine
whether the two triangles are
congruent. If they are, write a
congruence statement.

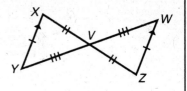

Proving Triangles are Congruent: SSS and SAS

Goal Show triangles are congruent using SSS and SAS.

VOCABULARY

Proof

POSTULATE 12: SIDE-SIDE-SIDE CONGRUENCE POSTULATE (SSS)

Words If three _____ of one triangle are congruent to three _____ of a second triangle, then the two triangles are _____.

Symbols If Side $\overline{MN} \cong \overline{QR}$, and

Side $\overline{NP} \cong \overline{RS}$, and

Side $\overline{PM} \cong \overline{SQ}$,

then $\triangle MNP \cong \triangle$ _____ .

Example 1 *Use the SSS Congruence Postulate*

Does the diagram give enough information to use the SSS Congruence Postulate? Explain.

Solution

From the diagram you know that $\overline{HJ} \cong$ ____ and $\overline{HK} \cong$ ____ .

By the _____ Property, you know that $\overline{JK} \cong \overline{JK}$.

Because all three pairs of corresponding sides are congruent, you can use the _____ Postulate to conclude that $\triangle HJK \cong \triangle$ _____ .

POSTULATE 13: SIDE-ANGLE-SIDE CONGRUENCE POSTULATE (SAS)

Words If two sides and the included angle of one triangle are congruent to two sides and the _____ angle of a second triangle, then the two triangles are _____.

Symbols If Side $\overline{PQ} \cong \overline{WX}$, and

       Angle $\angle Q \cong \angle X$, and

       Side $\overline{QR} \cong \overline{XY}$,

       then $\triangle PQR \cong \triangle$ _____.

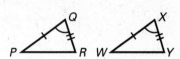

Example 2   *Use the SAS Congruence Postulate*

Does the diagram give enough information to use the SAS Congruence Postulate? Explain your reasoning.

a.

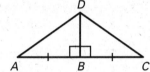

b.

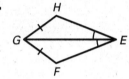

Solution

a. You know that $\overline{AB} \cong$ _____ and $\overline{DB} \cong$ _____.

The included angle between $\overline{AB}$ and $\overline{DB}$ is $\angle ABD$.

The included angle between $\overline{CB}$ and $\overline{DB}$ is $\angle$ _____.

Because the included angles are congruent, you can use the _____ Postulate to conclude that

$\triangle ABD \cong \triangle$ _____.

b. You know that $\overline{GF} \cong$ _____ and $\overline{GE} \cong$ _____ but the congruent

angles $\angle$ _____ and $\angle$ _____ are not included between the congruent sides, so you _____ use the SAS Congruence Postulate.

Follow-Up

In Example 2, part (b), what two angles must be congruent in order to use the SAS Congruence Postulate?

Checkpoint Does the diagram give enough information to determine whether the triangles are congruent?

1.	2.	3.

STEPS FOR WRITING A PROOF

• List the _____ information first.

• Decide whether you can use the given information as it is or if you need to make another statement based on the given information.

• List your statements in sequential order—in other words, don't list a conclusion before you list the statement that allows you to make that conclusion.

• Give a _____ for every statement that you make.

• As reasons in a proof, use given information, labeled diagrams, postulates, definitions, and theorems.

• End the proof with the statement you are trying to _____ .

Example 3 Write a Proof

Write a two-column proof that shows △*HJK* ≅ △*LKJ*.

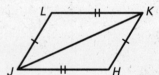

Solution

	Statements	Reasons
Side	1. $\overline{HJ}$ ≅ ____	1. Given
Side	2. $\overline{HK}$ ≅ ____	2. Given
Side	3. ____ ≅ ____	3. Reflexive Property of Congruen
	4. △*HJK* ≅ △*LKJ*	4. ____ Congruence Postulate

Example 4 *Prove Triangles are Congruent*

In the diagram at the right, $\overline{DR} \perp \overline{AG}$ and
$\overline{RA} \cong \overline{RG}$. Write a proof to show that
$\triangle DRA \cong \triangle DRG$.

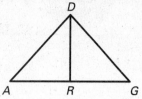

Solution

1. Label the diagram with the given information.

2. Write what you are given and what you need to prove.

    Given: _____ , _____

    Prove: _____

3. Write a two-column proof. List the given statements first.

Statements	Reasons
1. $\overline{RA} \cong \overline{RG}$	1. Given
2. $\overline{DR} \perp \overline{AG}$	2. Given
3. $\angle DRG$ and $\angle DRA$ are right angles.	3. Perpendicular lines form _____ angles.
4. $\angle DRG \cong \angle DRA$	4. All right angles are _____ .
5. ____ $\cong$ ____	5. Reflexive Property of Congruence
6. $\triangle$____ $\cong$ $\triangle$____	6. _____ Postulate

✔ *Checkpoint* Complete the proof.

4. **Given:** $\overline{CB} \cong \overline{CE}, \overline{AC} \cong \overline{DC}$
   Prove: $\triangle BCA \cong \triangle ECD$

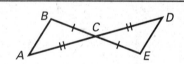

Statements	Reasons
1. $\overline{CB} \cong \overline{CE}$	1. _____
2. _____	2. Given
3. $\angle BCA \cong \angle ECD$	3. _____ Theorem
4. $\triangle BCA \cong \triangle ECD$	4. _____ Postulate

5.3 Proving Triangles are Congruent: ASA and AAS

Goal Show triangles are congruent using ASA and AAS.

POSTULATE 14: ANGLE-SIDE-ANGLE CONGRUENCE POSTULATE (ASA)

Words If two angles and the included side of one triangle are congruent to two angles and the included side of a second triangle, then the two triangles are _____.

Symbols

If Angle $\angle A \cong \angle D$, and
   Side $\overline{AC} \cong \overline{DF}$, and
   Angle $\angle C \cong \angle F$,
   then $\triangle ABC \cong \triangle$ _____.

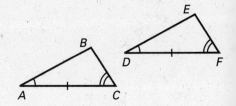

Follow-Up

Use $\triangle TGL$ shown. Complete the table.

Angles	Included Side
$\angle T$ and $\angle G$	
$\angle G$ and $\angle L$	
$\angle T$ and $\angle L$	

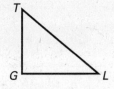

Draw any $\triangle ABC$ in the space below. Complete the table.

Angles	Non-Included Sides
$\angle A$ and $\angle B$	and
$\angle B$ and $\angle C$	and
$\angle A$ and $\angle C$	and

Example 1 **Determine When to Use ASA**

Based on the diagrams, can you use the ASA Congruence Postulate to show that the triangles are congruent? Explain.

a. 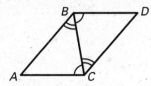   b.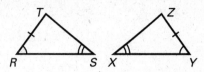

Solution

a. In △ABC, the included side between the marked angles is ____.

   In △DCB, the included side is ____. These sides are congruent by the _____ Property. So, with ∠ACB ≅ ∠____, ∠ABC ≅ ∠____, and ____ ≅ ____, you can use the ASA Congruence Postulate to show that △ABC ≅ △DCB.

b. In △RST, the included side is ____. In △YXZ, the included side is ____. Since these sides are not marked congruent, you cannot use the ASA Congruence Postulate.

THEOREM 5.1: ANGLE-ANGLE-SIDE CONGRUENCE THEOREM (AAS)

Words If two angles and a non-included side of one triangle are congruent to two angles and the corresponding non-included side of a second triangle, then the two triangles are _____.

Symbols

   If Angle   ∠A ≅ ∠D, and
      Angle   ∠C ≅ ∠F, and
      Side $\overline{BC} \cong \overline{EF}$,
   then △ABC ≅ △____.

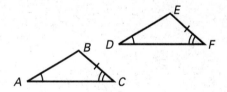

Follow-Up

In Example 1, part (b), can you use the AAS Congruence Theorem to show that the triangles are congruent?

Example 2 **Determine What Information is Missing**

What additional congruence is needed to show that △*JKL* ≅ △*NML* by the AAS Congruence Theorem?

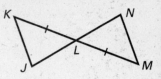

Solution

You are given $\overline{KL}$ ≅ $\overline{ML}$. You know ∠*KLJ* ≅ ∠*MLN* because they are _____ angles. The angles that make $\overline{KL}$ and $\overline{ML}$ the non-included sides are ∠___ and ∠___. So, to use the AAS Congruence Theorem you need the congruence _____.

Example 3 **Decide Whether Triangles are Congruent**

Does the diagram give enough information to show that the triangles are congruent? If so, state the postulate or theorem you would use.

a. 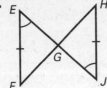 **b.** 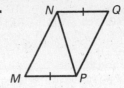 **c.**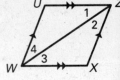

Solution

a. Use the _____ Congruence Theorem.

    Side   ____ ≅ ____ is given.

    Angle   ____ ≅ ____ is given.

    Angle   _____ ≅ _____ since vertical angles are congrue

b. You only know that $\overline{MP}$ ≅ $\overline{QN}$ and $\overline{NP}$ ≅ $\overline{NP}$. You _____ conclude that the triangles are congruent.

c. Use the _____ Congruence Postulate.

    Angle   ___ ≅ ___ since alternate interior angles are congruent.

    Angle   ___ ≅ ___ since alternate interior angles are congruent.

    Side   ____ ≅ ____ by the Reflexive Property of Congrue

Example 4   *Prove Triangles are Congruent*

Use the information given in the
diagram to prove △ABD ≅ △EBC.

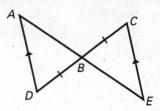

Solution

Given $\overline{AD} \parallel \overline{EC}$, $\overline{BD} \cong \overline{BC}$

Prove △ABD ≅ △EBC

Statements	Reasons
1. $\overline{BD} \cong \overline{BC}$	1. _____
2. _____	2. Given
3. ∠D ≅ ∠C	3. _____ Angles Theorem
4. ∠ABD ≅ ∠EBC	4. _____ Angles Theorem
5. _____	5. _____

Follow-Up

In Example 4, how can you use the AAS Congruence Theorem to
prove that the triangles are congruent?

✔ **Checkpoint** Does the diagram give enough information to show
that the triangles are congruent? If so, state the postulate or
theorem you would use.

1.	2.	3.

5.4 Hypotenuse-Leg Congruence Theorem: HL

Goal Use the HL Congruence Theorem and summarize congruence postulates and theorems.

THEOREM 5.2: HYPOTENUSE-LEG THEOREM

Words If the hypotenuse and leg of a _____ triangle are congruent to the hypotenuse and leg of a second _____ triangle, then the two triangles are _____.

Symbols If △ABC and △DEF are _____ triangles, and

H $\overline{AC} \cong \overline{DF}$, and
L $\overline{BC} \cong \overline{EF}$,
then △ABC ≅ △_____.

Follow-Up

In the space at the right, draw a right triangle with hypotenuse $\overline{RT}$ and leg $\overline{TG}$.

Name the other leg.

Example 1 *Determine When To Use HL*

Is it possible to show △GJH ≅ △KHJ using the HL Theorem? Explain your reasoning.

Solution

Yes. The diagram shows that △GJH and △KHJ are _____ triangles. In △GJH, the hypotenuse is $\overline{JH}$. In △KHJ, the hypotenuse is $\overline{JH}$. These hypoten____ are congruent by the _____ Property. The legs that are ma___ congruent are $\overline{JG}$ and $\overline{HK}$. So, you can use the _____ Theorem to show △GJH ≅ △KHJ.

Follow-Up Mark the diagrams with the information needed to show
$\triangle ABC \cong \triangle DEF$ using the congruence postulate or theorem.

SSS	Side	$\overline{AB} \cong \overline{DE}$	
	Side	$\overline{AC} \cong \overline{DF}$	
	Side	$\overline{BC} \cong \overline{EF}$	
SAS	Side	$\overline{AB} \cong \overline{DE}$	
	Angle	$\angle B \cong \angle E$	
	Side	$\overline{BC} \cong \overline{EF}$	
ASA	Angle	$\angle A \cong \angle D$	
	Side	$\overline{AB} \cong \overline{DE}$	
	Angle	$\angle B \cong \angle E$	
AAS	Angle	$\angle A \cong \angle D$	
	Angle	$\angle B \cong \angle E$	
	Side	$\overline{BC} \cong \overline{EF}$	
HL	$\triangle ABC$ and $\triangle DEF$ are right triangles.		
	Hypotenuse	$\overline{AB} \cong \overline{DE}$	
	Leg	$\overline{BC} \cong \overline{EF}$	

Example 2 **Use the HL Theorem**

Use the information in the diagram
to prove $\triangle PRQ \cong \triangle PRS$.

Solution

Given $\overline{PR} \perp \overline{SQ}$, $\overline{PS} \cong \overline{PQ}$

Prove $\triangle PRQ \cong \triangle PRS$

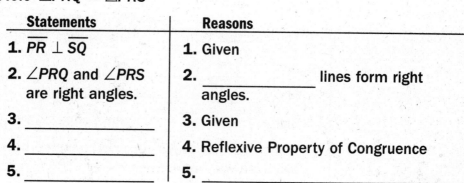

Statements	Reasons
1. $\overline{PR} \perp \overline{SQ}$	1. Given
2. $\angle PRQ$ and $\angle PRS$ are right angles.	2. _____ lines form right angles.
3. _____	3. Given
4. _____	4. Reflexive Property of Congruence
5. _____	5. _____

In Example 2, why are the first two steps of the proof necessary?

_____

Which step shows that two hypotenuses are congruent?

_____

Which step shows that two legs are congruent?

Example 3   *Decide Whether Triangles are Congruent*

Does the diagram give enough information to prove that the triangles are congruent? If so, state the postulate or theorem you would use.

a.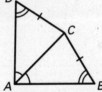

b.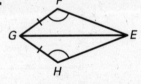

Solution

List the congruent sides and angles and see if there is a theorem postulate you can use.

a. Angle _____ ≅ _____ is given.

   Angle ____ ≅ ____ is given.

   Side ____ ≅ ____ is given.

   You can use the _____ Congruence Theorem.

b. Side ____ ≅ ____ is given.

   Angle ____ ≅ ____ is given.

   Side ____ ≅ ____ by the Reflexive Property.

The congruent angles are not included between the congruent sides, so you cannot use _____. There is no SSA congruence postulate or theorem.

Example 4 **Prove Triangles are Congruent**

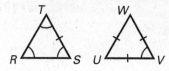

Prove that $\triangle RST \cong \triangle UVW$.

Solution

Statements	Reasons
1. $\overline{ST} \cong \overline{VW}$	1. _____
2. $\angle S \cong \angle V$; $\angle T \cong \angle V$	2. _____
3. $\triangle UVW$ is equilateral.	3. Definition of _____ triangle
4. $\angle V \cong \angle W$	4. Equilateral triangles are _____.
5. $\angle T \cong \angle W$	5. Transitive Property of _____
6. _____	6. ASA Congruence Postulate

Follow-Up

Write three congruence statements to show how the Transitive Property is used in Example 4.

_____

Write three congruence statements to show how the ASA Congruence Postulate is used in Example 4.

✓ *Checkpoint* Does the diagram give enough information to show that the triangles are congruent? If so, state the postulate or theorem you would use.

1.	2.	3.
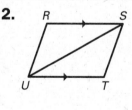		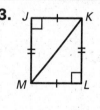

5.5 Using Congruent Triangles

Goal Show corresponding parts of congruent triangles are congruent.

Example 1 *Show Corresponding Parts are Congruent*

In the diagram, $\overline{AB}$ and $\overline{CD}$ bisect each other at M. Prove that $\angle A \cong \angle B$.

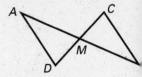

Solution

Mark any congruent segments or angles on the diagram.

Because $\angle A$ and $\angle B$ are corresponding angles in $\triangle ADM$ and $\triangle \_\_\_$, show that $\triangle ADM \cong \triangle \_\_\_\_$ to prove $\angle A \cong \angle B$.

Statements	Reasons
1. $\overline{AB}$ and $\overline{CD}$ bisect each other at M.	1. _____
2. $\overline{MA} \cong \overline{MB}$	2. Definition of segment bisector
3. $\angle AMD \cong \angle BMC$	3. _____
4. $\overline{MD} \cong \overline{MC}$	4. _____
5. $\triangle ADM \cong \triangle \_\_\_\_$	5. _____
6. _____	6. Corresponding parts of $\cong$ triangles are $\cong$.

Example 2 **Visualize Overlapping Triangles**

Sketch the overlapping triangles separately. Mark all congruent angles and sides. Then tell what theorem or postulate you can use to show △JGH ≅ △KHG.

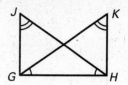

Solution

1. Sketch the triangles separately, moving △JGH to the left and △KHG to the right. Mark the congruent angles, which are given on the original diagram.

2. Look for shared sides, shared angles, and any other information you can deduce.

   Which side is the same in both triangles? _____

   Mark these congruent sides on your diagram above.

3. Look again at your marked diagram. You can use the _____ Congruence Theorem to show △JGH ≅ △KHG.

Follow-Up

Redraw each diagram so that the triangles do not overlap. Label the vertices and mark any congruent sides or angles.

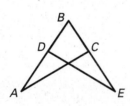

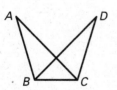

Example 3   *Use Overlapping Triangles*

In the diagram, $\overline{CB} \cong \overline{CE}$ and $\angle DEC \cong \angle ABC$.
Prove that $\overline{AB} \cong \overline{DE}$.

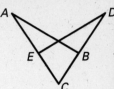

Solution

Which triangles do you need to prove
are congruent in order to prove $\overline{AB} \cong \overline{DE}$? _____ $\cong$ _____

Use the space below to sketch the triangles separately. Then label
the given information and any other information you can deduce.
Which angle is the same in both triangles? _____

Statements	Reasons
1. _____	1. Given
2. $\overline{CB}$ ___ ____	2. Given
3. _____	3. Reflexive Property of Congruence
4. $\triangle ABC \cong \triangle DEC$	4. _____
5. $\overline{AB}$ ___ ____	5. _____

✔ Checkpoint Redraw the triangles separately and label all congruent parts. Then show that the triangles or corresponding parts are congruent.

---

1. Given $\overline{KJ} \cong \overline{KL}$ and $\angle J \cong \angle L$, show $\overline{NJ} \cong \overline{ML}$.

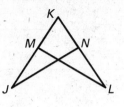

---

2. Given $\angle SPR \cong \angle QRP$ and $\angle Q \cong \angle S$, show $\triangle PQR \cong \triangle RSP$.

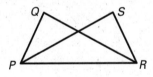

5.6 Angle Bisectors and Perpendicular Bisectors

Goal Use angle bisectors and perpendicular bisectors.

VOCABULARY

Distance from a point to a line

Equidistant

Perpendicular bisector

THEOREM 5.3: ANGLE BISECTOR THEOREM

Words If a point is on the bisector of an angle, then it is
_____ from the two sides of the angle.

If 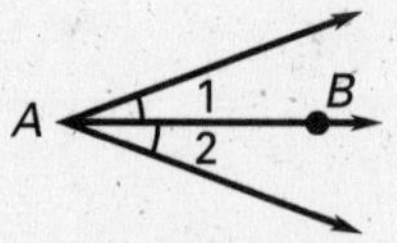   then

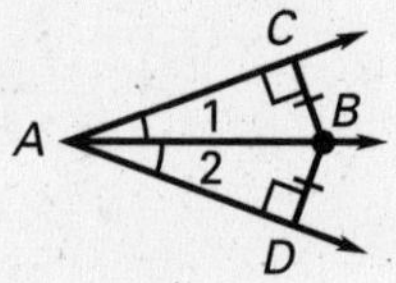

Symbols If $m\angle 1 = m\angle 2$, then _____ .

Example 1 *Use the Angle Bisector Theorem*

In the diagram, $\overrightarrow{UW}$ bisects $\angle TUV$.
$\angle UTW$ and $\angle UVW$ are right angles.
Prove that $\triangle TWU \cong \triangle VWU$.

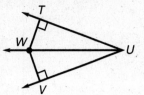

Solution

Statements	Reasons
1. $\overrightarrow{UW}$ bisects $\angle TUV$.	1. _____
2. $\angle$ _____ $\cong \angle$ _____	2. Definition of angle bisector
3. $\overline{WT} \cong \overline{WV}$	3. Angle Bisector Theorem
4. $\angle UTW$ and $\angle UVW$ right angles.	4. _____
5. $\angle UTW \cong \angle UVW$	5. Right angles are _____.
6. $\triangle TWU \cong \triangle VWU$	6. _____

Follow-Up

Write three congruence statements to show how the
AAS Congruence Theorem is used in Example 1.

THEOREM 5.4: PERPENDICULAR BISECTOR THEOREM

Words If a point is on the perpendicular bisector of a segment,
then it is _____ from the endpoints of the segment.

If

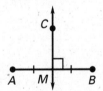

then

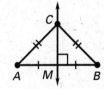

Symbols If C is on the perpendicular bisector of $\overline{AB}$, then
_____.

Example 2　Use Perpendicular Bisectors

Use the diagram to find *AB*.

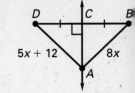

Solution

$\overleftrightarrow{AC}$ is the perpendicular bisector of $\overline{DB}$
because $\overleftrightarrow{AC} \perp \overline{DB}$ and $\overline{DC} \cong \overline{BC}$. The
Perpendicular Bisector Theorem tells you _____ .

$8x =$ _____ 　　　**Perpendicular Bisector Theorem**

_____ $=$ _____ 　　　**Subtract ____ from each side.**

$x =$ __ 　　　　　**Divide each side by __ .**

Answer $AB =$. $8x = 8(\_\_) =$ ____

Follow-Up

Check your answer in Example 2 by finding *AD*.

$AD = 5x + 12 = 5(\_\_) + 12 =$ ___ .

Does *AB* equal *AD*? _____

✔ *Checkpoint* **Find the indicated measure.**

1. Find *FH*.	**2.** Find *MK*.	**3.** Find *EF*.
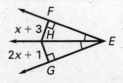	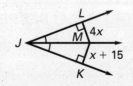	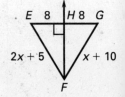

Example 3　Use the Perpendicular Bisector Theorem

In the diagram, $\overleftrightarrow{MN}$ is the perpendicular bisector of $\overline{ST}$. Prove that $\triangle MST$ is an isosceles triangle.

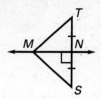

Solution

Statements	Reasons
1. $\overleftrightarrow{MN}$ is the ⊥ bisector of $\overline{ST}$.	1. _____
2. $\overline{MS} \cong \overline{MT}$	2. Perpendicular Bisector Theorem
3. $\triangle MST$ is isosceles.	3. Definition of _____

Example 4　Use Intersecting Bisectors of a Triangle

A company plans to build a warehouse that is equally close to each of its three stores, A, B, and C. Where should the warehouse be built?

•B

Solution

1. On the diagram, connect points to draw $\triangle ABC$.

A•

2. Draw the perpendicular bisectors of $\overline{AB}$, $\overline{BC}$, and $\overline{CA}$. Label point P, the intersection of the bisectors.

•C

Answer The warehouse should be built at point P because ____ = ____ = ____ .

5.7 Reflections and Symmetry

Goal Identify and use reflections and lines of symmetry.

VOCABULARY

Reflection

Line of symmetry

PROPERTIES OF REFLECTIONS

1. The reflected image is _____ to the original figure.

2. The orientation of the reflected image is _____.

3. The line of reflection is the _____ of the segments joining the corresponding points.

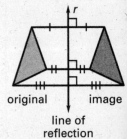

original   image

line of reflection

Follow-Up

Draw the reflection of the letter E in line *k*.

Example 1 *Identify Reflections*

Tell whether the gray figure is a reflection of the black figure in line *m*.

a.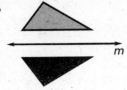

b.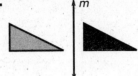

Solution

Check to see if all three properties of a reflection are met.

a. Is the image congruent to the original figure? _____

   Is the orientation of the image reversed? _____

   Are the lines connecting the corresponding points perpendicular to line *m*? _____

   Yes, the gray triangle is a reflection of the black triangle because

   _____ .

b. Is the image congruent to the original figure? _____

   Is the orientation of the image reversed? _____

   Are the lines connecting the corresponding points perpendicular to line *m*? _____

   No, the gray triangle is not a reflection of the black triangle because _____ .

Follow-Up

Name the transformation shown in Example 1, part (b).

Example 2 **Reflections in a Coordinate Plane**

a. Which segment is the reflection of $\overline{AB}$ in the x-axis? Which point corresponds to A? to B?

b. Which segment is a reflection of $\overline{AB}$ in the y-axis? Which point corresponds to A? to B?

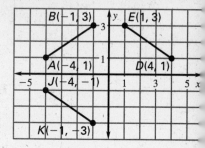

Solution

a. The x-axis is perpendicular to $\overline{AJ}$ and $\overline{BK}$, so the reflection of $\overline{AB}$ in the x-axis is _____.

A is reflected onto ___. $A(-4, 1) \rightarrow$ _____

B is reflected onto ___. $B(-1, 3) \rightarrow$ _____

b. The y-axis is perpendicular to $\overline{AD}$ and $\overline{BE}$, so the reflection of $\overline{AB}$ in the y-axis is _____.

A is reflected onto ___. $A(-4, 1) \rightarrow$ _____

B is reflected onto ___. $B(-1, 3) \rightarrow$ _____

✓ *Checkpoint* **Tell whether the gray figure is a reflection of the black figure. If it is a reflection, tell the line of reflection.**

1.

2.

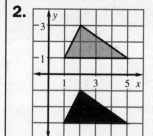

3.

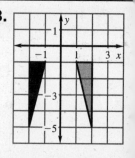

Example 3 *Find Lines of Symmetry*

Determine the number of lines of symmetry in each figure.

a.

b.

c.

Solution

Draw the lines of symmetry on the figures and count them.

a. __

b. __

c. __

Follow-Up Is the following statement *true* or *false*?

> A line of symmetry is also a line of reflection.

Example 4 *Use Lines of Symmetry*

Inside a kaleidoscope, two mirrors are placed to form a V. The angle A between the mirrors is related to the number n of lines of symmetry in a pattern by the equation $m\angle A = \dfrac{180°}{n}$. Find the angle between the mirrors for each kaleidoscope design.

a.

b.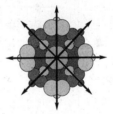

Solution

a. The design has __ lines of symmetry, so $n = $ __.

$$m\angle A = \frac{180°}{n} = \underline{} = \underline{}°.$$

b. The design has __ lines of symmetry, so $n = $ __.

$$m\angle A = \frac{180°}{n} = \underline{} = \underline{}°.$$

Words to Review

Give an example of the vocabulary word.

Corresponding parts	Congruent figures
Distance from a point to a line	**Equidistant**
Perpendicular bisector	

Review your notes and Chapter 5 by using the Chapter Summary and Review on pages 291–295 of your textbook.

6.1 Polygons

Goal Identify and describe polygons. Find angle measures of quadrilaterals.

VOCABULARY

Polygon, side, vertex

Diagonal of a polygon

Follow-Up

Draw any polygon *ABCD*.

Name all the vertices. _____

Name all the sides. _____

Name all the diagonals. _____

Example 1 *Identify Polygons*

Is the figure a polygon? Explain your reasoning.

a.

b.

c.

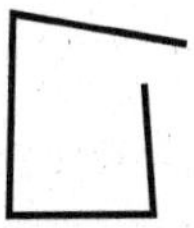

Solution

a. Yes. The figure is a polygon formed by ___ straight sides.

b. No. The figure is not a polygon because _____
_____.

c. No. The figure is not a polygon because _____
_____.

Follow-Up For each type of polygon, write the number of sides. Then sketch the polygon described.

Triangle ___ sides	**Hexagon** ___ sides
Quadrilateral ___ sides	**Heptagon** ___ sides
Pentagon ___ sides	**Octagon** ___ sides

Example 2 *Describe Polygons*

Decide whether the figure is a polygon. If so, tell what type. If not, explain why.

a. b. c.

Solution

a. Yes. The figure is a polygon with ___ sides, so it is a

_____.

b. Yes. The figure is a polygon with ___ sides, so it is a _____

c. No. The figure is not a polygon because _____

_____.

Checkpoint Decide whether the figure is a polygon. If so, tell what type. If not, explain why.

1.	2.	3.

THEOREM 6.1: QUADRILATERAL INTERIOR ANGLES THEOREM

Words The sum of the measures of the angles of a quadrilateral is ____°.

Symbols $m\angle 1 + m\angle 2 + m\angle 3 + m\angle 4 =$ ____°

Follow-Up Draw quadrilateral *ABCD* and divide it into two triangles by drawing diagonal $\overline{AC}$.

The sum of the angle measures of △*ABC* is ____° and the sum of the angle measures of △*ACD* is ____°.

So, the sum of the angle measures of *ABCD* is ____° + ____° = ____°.

Example 3   *Find Angle Measures of Quadrilaterals*

Find the measure of ∠*S*.

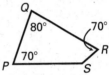

Solution

$m\angle P + m\angle Q + m\angle R + m\angle S =$ ____°   **Quadrilateral Interior Angles Theorem**

____° + ____° + ____° + $m\angle S =$ ____°   **Substitute angle measures.**

____° + $m\angle S =$ ____°   **Simplify.**

$m\angle S =$ ____°   **Solve for $m\angle S$.**

✔ **Checkpoint** Find the measure of ∠*A*.

4.

B 110°   60° *C*
A 100° *D*

5.

C 55°
160° *D*
B 80° *A*

6.

B 72° *A*
C 108° 108° *D*

6.2 Properties of Parallelograms

Goal Use properties of parallelograms.

VOCABULARY

Parallelogram

THEOREM 6.2

Words If a quadrilateral is a parallelogram,
then its _____ sides are congruent.

Symbols In □PQRS, $\overline{PQ} \cong$ ____ and
$\overline{QR} \cong$ ____ .

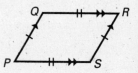

Example 1 *Find Side Lengths of Parallelograms*

FGHJ is a parallelogram.
Find JH and FJ.

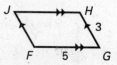

Solution

Opposite sides of a parallelogram are congruent.

$JH = FG =$ ____ $FJ = GH =$ ____

✓ **Checkpoint** Complete the following exercise.

---

1. ABCD is a parallelogram.
Find AB and AD.

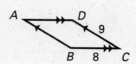

THEOREM 6.3

Words If a quadrilateral is a parallelogram, then its _____ angles are congruent.

Symbols In ▱PQRS, ∠P ≅ ∠___ and ∠Q ≅ ∠___.

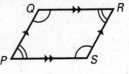

THEOREM 6.4

Words If a quadrilateral is a parallelogram, then its consecutive angles are

_____ .

Symbols In ▱PQRS, $x° + y° =$ ___°.

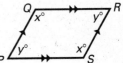

Follow-Up

Use the words in the box at the right to make two true statements about parallelograms.

_____ angles are _____ .

_____ angles are _____ .

congruent
consecutive
opposite
supplementary

Example 2 *Find Angle Measures of Parallelograms*

PQRS is a parallelogram.
Find the missing angle measures.

Solution

Opposite angles of a parallelogram are congruent.

$m∠R = m∠$___ $=$ ___°

Consecutive angles of a parallelogram are supplementary.

$m∠Q + m∠P =$ ____°   Write an equation.

$m∠Q +$ ___° $=$ ___°   Substitute for $m∠P$.

$m∠Q =$ ___°   Solve for $m∠Q$.

Opposite angles of a parallelogram are congruent.

$m∠S = m∠Q =$ ___°

Answer $m∠R =$ ___°, $m∠Q =$ ___°, $m∠S =$ ___°

Follow-Up

Estimate the angle measures
in □*WXYZ*.

$m\angle W =$ _____ $^\circ$ $m\angle X =$ _____ $^\circ$

$m\angle Y =$ _____ $^\circ$ $m\angle Z =$ _____ $^\circ$

What is the sum of the angle measures?

✓ **Checkpoint** *ABCD* **is a parallelogram. Find the missing angle measures.**

2.

3.

THEOREM 6.5

Words If a quadrilateral is a parallelogram,
then its _____ bisect each other.

Symbols In □*PQRS*, $\overline{QM} \cong$ _____ and
$\overline{PM} \cong$ _____ .

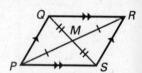

Example 3   *Find Segment Lengths*

TUVW is a parallelogram.
Find *TX*.

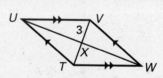

Solution

The diagonals of a parallelogram bisect each other.

$TX =$ _____ $=$ _____

6.3 Showing Quadrilaterals are Parallelograms

Goal Show that a quadrilateral is a parallelogram.

THEOREM 6.6

Words If both pairs of opposite sides of a quadrilateral are congruent, then the quadrilateral is a _____.

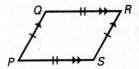

Symbols If $\overline{PQ} \cong \overline{SR}$ and $\overline{QR} \cong \overline{PS}$, then PQRS is a _____.

THEOREM 6.7

Words If both pairs of opposite angles of a quadrilateral are congruent, then the quadrilateral is a _____.

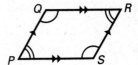

Symbols If $\angle P \cong \angle R$ and $\angle Q \cong \angle S$, then PQRS is a _____.

Follow-Up

Write the converse of Theorem 6.6. Is the converse true or false? How do you know?

_____

Write the converse of Theorem 6.7. Is the converse true or false? How do you know?

Lesson 6.3 · **Geometry, Concepts and Skills Notetaking Guide**   **141**

Example 1   *Use Theorems 6.6 and 6.7*

Tell whether the quadrilateral is a parallelogram. Explain.

a.

b.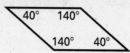

Solution

a. No. The quadrilateral is not a parallelogram because it has two pairs of congruent sides, but _____

_____.

b. Yes. The quadrilateral is a parallelogram because _____

_____.

THEOREM 6.8

Words If an angle of a quadrilateral is _____ to both of its consecutive angles, then the quadrilateral is a parallelogram.

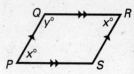

Symbols If $m\angle P + m\angle Q =$ _____$°$ and $m\angle Q + m\angle R =$ _____$°$, then *PQRS* is a parallelogram.

THEOREM 6.9

Words If the diagonals of a quadrilateral _____, then the quadrilateral is a parallelogram.

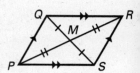

Symbols If $\overline{QM} \cong$ _____ and $\overline{PM} \cong$ _____, then *PQRS* is a parallelogram.

Follow-Up

Write the converse of Theorem 6.8. Is the converse true or false? How do you know?

Example 2   *Use Theorems 6.8 and 6.9*

Tell whether the quadrilateral is a parallelogram. Explain your reasoning.

a.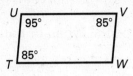

b.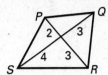

Solution

a. Yes. This quadrilateral is a parallelogram because _____

_____

b. No. This quadrilateral is not a parallelogram because _____

_____

✔ *Checkpoint* Tell whether the quadrilateral is a parallelogram. Explain your reasoning.

1.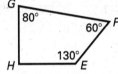

2.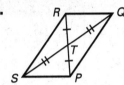

3.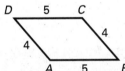

4.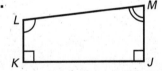

6.4 Rhombuses, Rectangles, and Squares

Goal Use properties of special types of parallelograms.

VOCABULARY

Rhombus

Rectangle

Square

Example 1 *Use Properties of Special Parallelograms*

In the diagram, *ABCD* is a rectangle.

a. Find *AD* and *AB*.

b. Find *m∠A*, *m∠B*, *m∠C*, and *m∠D*.

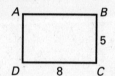

Solution

a. By definition, a rectangle is a parallelogram, so *ABCD* is a parallelogram. Because opposite sides of a parallelogram are _____, *AD* = ____ = ___ and *AB* = ____ = ___.

b. By definition, a rectangle has four right angles, so *m∠A* = *m∠B* = *m∠C* = *m∠D* = ___°.

✔ **Checkpoint** Complete the following exercise.

---

1. In the diagram, *PQRS* is a rhombus. Find *QR*, *RS*, and *SP*.

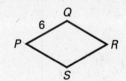

RHOMBUS COROLLARY

Words If a quadrilateral has _____
_____ , then it is a rhombus.

Symbols If $\overline{AB} \cong \overline{BC} \cong \overline{CD} \cong \overline{AD}$, then $ABCD$ is
a rhombus.

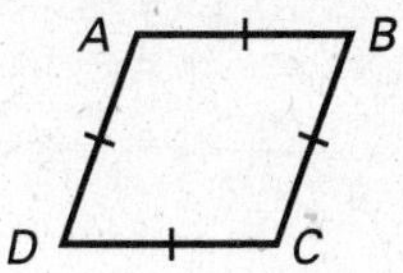

RECTANGLE COROLLARY

Words If a quadrilateral has _____ ,
then it is a rectangle.

Symbols If $m\angle A = m\angle B = m\angle C = m\angle D = 90°$,
then $ABCD$ is a rectangle.

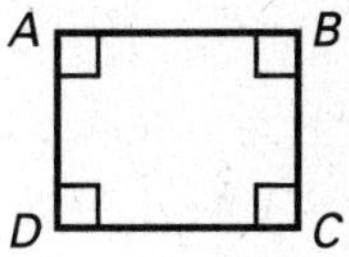

SQUARE COROLLARY

Words If a quadrilateral has _____
and _____ , then it is a square.

Symbols If $\overline{AB} \cong \overline{BC} \cong \overline{CD} \cong \overline{AD}$ and
$m\angle A = m\angle B = m\angle C = m\angle D = 90°$, then $ABCD$ is
a square.

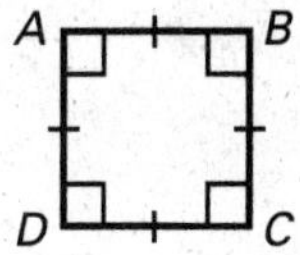

Example 2 *Identify Special Parallelograms*

Use the information in the diagram
to name the special quadrilateral.

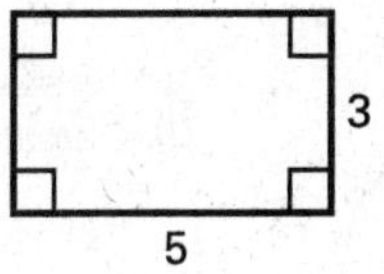

Solution

The quadrilateral has four _____ . So, by the _____
Corollary, the quadrilateral is a _____ .

Because all of the sides are not the same length, you know that the
quadrilateral is not a _____ .

2.

3.

THEOREM 6.10

Words The diagonals of a rhombus are _____.

Symbols In rhombus $ABCD$, $\overline{AC} \perp \overline{BD}$.

Example 3 *Use Diagonals of a Rhombus*

$ABCD$ is a rhombus. Find the value of x.

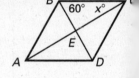

Solution

By Theorem 6.10, the diagonals of a rhombus are _____. Therefore, $\angle BEC$ is a _____ angle, so $\triangle BEC$ is a _____ triangle.

By the Corollary to the Triangle Sum Theorem, the acute angles o _____ triangle are _____. So, $x =$ ___ − ___ = __

THEOREM 6.11

Words The diagonals of a rectangle are _____.

Symbols In rectangle $ABCD$, $\overline{AC} \cong \overline{BD}$.

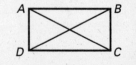

Example 4 *Use Special Properties of Parallelograms*

a. You nail four pieces of wood together to build a four-sided frame, as shown. What is the shape of the frame?

b. The diagonals measure 7 ft 4 in. and 7 ft 2 in. Is the frame a rectangle?

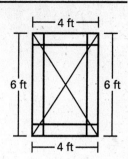

Solution

a. The frame is a _____ because both pairs of opposite sides are congruent.

b. No. The frame is not a rectangle because _____

_____ .

Follow-Up

Which theorem did you use in Example 4, part (b)?

✔ *Checkpoint* ABCD has the properties shown in the figure. Is the statement *true* or *false*? Explain.

4. ABCD is a rhombus.

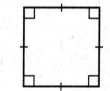

_____

5. ABCD is a parallelogram.

_____

6. ABCD is a rectangle.

_____

7. The diagonals are congruent.

6.5 Trapezoids

Goal Use properties of trapezoids.

VOCABULARY

Trapezoid

Bases of a trapezoid

Legs of a trapezoid

Base angles of a trapezoid

Isosceles trapezoid

Midsegment of a trapezoid

THEOREM 6.12

Words If a trapezoid is isosceles, then each pair of base angles is _____ .

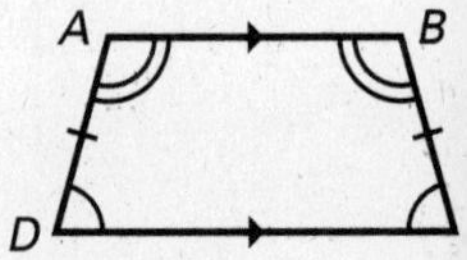

Symbols In the isosceles trapezoid ABCD,
$\angle A \cong \angle \underline{}$ and $\angle C \cong \angle \underline{}$.

THEOREM 6.13

Words If a trapezoid has a pair of _____ base angles, then it is isosceles.

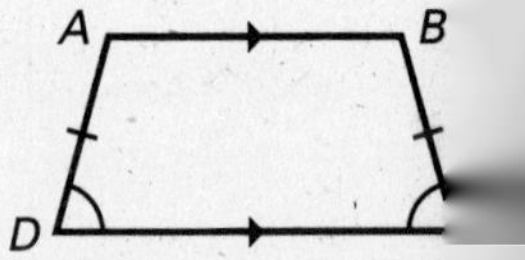

Symbols In trapezoid ABCD, if $\angle C \cong \angle D$ then ABCD is isosceles.

Follow-Up Tell whether the statement is true for *isosceles triangles*, *isosceles trapezoids*, *both*, or *neither*.

Legs are congruent. _____

Base angles are congruent. _____

Bases are parallel. _____

Legs are parallel. _____

Example 1 *Find Angle Measures of Trapezoids*

PQRS is an isosceles trapezoid.
Find the missing angle measures.

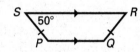

Solution

1. Use Theorem 6.12. *PQRS* is an isosceles trapezoid. ∠R and ∠S are a pair of _____ angles. So, $m\angle R = m\angle\_\_\_ = \_\_\_$°.

2. Use the Same-Side Interior Angles Theorem. In the trapezoid, $\overline{SR} \parallel \overline{PQ}$ cut by transversal $\overline{SP}$. Since ∠S and ∠P are same-side interior angles, they are _____. So, $m\angle P = \_\_\_$° $- \_\_\_$° $= \_\_\_$°.

3. Use Theorem 6.12. *PQRS* is an isosceles trapezoid. ∠P and ∠Q are a pair of _____ angles. So, $m\angle Q = m\angle\_\_\_ = \_\_\_$°.

✓ **Checkpoint** *ABCD* is an isosceles trapezoid. Find the missing angle measures.

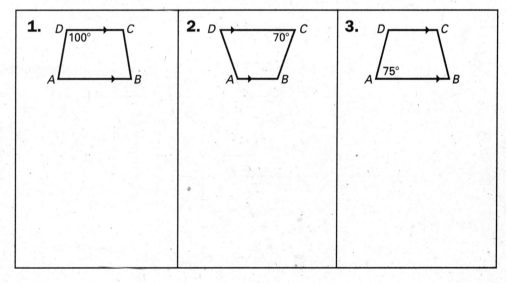

MIDSEGMENT OF A TRAPEZOID

The length of the midsegment of a
trapezoid is _____

_____ .

$$MN = \frac{1}{2}(AD + BC)$$

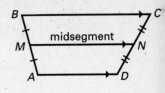

Example 2   *Midsegment of a Trapezoid*

Find the length of the midsegment $\overline{DG}$
of trapezoid *CEFH*.

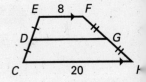

Solution

Use the formula for the midsegment of
a trapezoid.

$$DG = \frac{1}{2}(EF + CH) = \frac{1}{2}(\underline{\ \ } + \underline{\ \ }) = \frac{1}{2}(\underline{\ \ }) = \underline{\ \ }$$

Answer The length of the midsegment $\overline{DG}$ is ___ .

Follow-Up

In the space at the right, draw any
trapezoid *TPZD* with midsegment $\overline{MS}$ so
that the equation $MS = \frac{1}{2}(TP + ZD)$ is
true. Mark all parallel sides and
congruent segments.

✔ *Checkpoint* Find the length of the midsegment $\overline{MN}$.

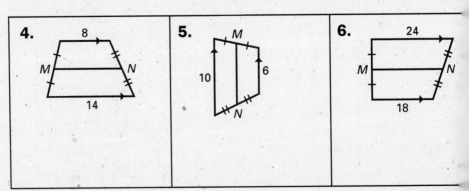

4.   8, 14

5.   10, 6

6.   24, 18

Reasoning About Special Quadrilaterals

Goal Identify special quadrilaterals based on limited information.

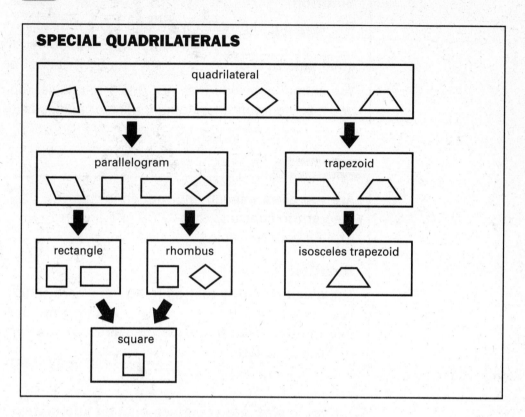

SPECIAL QUADRILATERALS

Follow-Up **Complete each statement.**

A square is always a _____, a _____, a _____, and a _____.

A rectangle is always a _____ and a _____.

A rhombus is always a _____ and a _____.

A parallelogram is always a _____.

An isosceles trapezoid is always a _____ and a _____.

A trapezoid is always a _____.

Example 1   *Use Properties of Quadrilaterals*

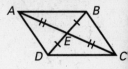

Determine whether the quadrilateral is a
parallelogram, trapezoid, rectangle, rhombus,
or *square.*

Solution

The diagram shows $\overline{CE} \cong \overline{EA}$ and $\overline{DE} \cong \overline{EB}$, so _____
_____ . By Theorem 6.9, you know that the
quadrilateral is a _____ . So it cannot be a trapezoid.

You cannot conclude that *ABCD* is a rectangle, rhombus, or square
because no information about sides or angles is given.

Example 2   *Identify a Rhombus*

Are you given enough information in the
diagram to conclude that *ABCD* is a square?
Explain your reasoning.

Solution

The diagram shows that all four _____ are congruent. Therefore,
you know that it is a _____ . The diagram does not give any
information about the angle measures, so you cannot conclude tha
ABCD is a square.

✔ *Checkpoint* Are you given enough information to conclude tha
    the figure is the given type of special quadrilateral? Explain
    your reasoning.

1. A square?

2. A rhombus?

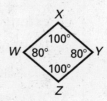

Example 3 *Identify a Trapezoid*

Are you given enough information in the diagram to conclude that *EFGH* is an isosceles trapezoid? Explain your reasoning.

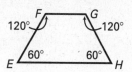

Solution

1. First show that *EFGH* is a trapezoid.

   ∠*E* and ∠*F* are _____, so $\overline{FG}$ and $\overline{EH}$ are _____ by the Same-Side Interior Angles Converse. So, *EFGH* has at least one pair of parallel sides.

   To show that *EFGH* is a trapezoid, you must show that *EFGH* does not have a second pair of parallel sides. In other words, show that *EFGH* is not a _____. Opposite angles of *EFGH* are not _____, so it cannot be a parallelogram. So, *EFGH* is a _____.

2. Next show that it is an isosceles trapezoid.

   Use Theorem 6.13. _____ are congruent, so *EFGH* is an isosceles trapezoid.

Follow-Up Describe one way to show that a quadrilateral is the given special type of quadrilateral.

Square

_____

Rhombus

_____

Rectangle

_____

Trapezoid

_____

Isosceles trapezoid

_____

Parallelogram

Words to Review

Give an example of the vocabulary word.

Polygon	Sides of a polygon
Vertex of a polygon	Diagonal of a polygon
Parallelogram	Rhombus
Rectangle	Square

Trapezoid	Bases of a trapezoid
Legs of a trapezoid	Base angles of a trapezoid
Isosceles trapezoid	Midsegment of a trapezoid

Review your notes and Chapter 6 by using the Chapter Summary and Review on pages 342–345 of your textbook.

7.1 Ratio and Proportion

Goal Use ratios and proportions.

VOCABULARY

Ratio

Proportion

Means

Extremes

Example 1 *Simplify Ratios*

Simplify the ratio.

a. 60 cm : 200 cm

b. $\dfrac{3 \text{ ft}}{18 \text{ in.}}$

Solution

a. 60 cm : 200 cm can be written as the fraction $\dfrac{60 \text{ cm}}{200 \text{ cm}}$.

Divide the numerator and the denominator by their greatest common factor, 20.

$$\frac{60 \text{ cm}}{200 \text{ cm}} = \underline{\hspace{2cm}} = \underline{\hspace{1.5cm}}$$

b. Before you can simplify this ratio, the quantities in the numera
and denominator must be written in the same units. To use
inches, substitute 12 in. for 1 ft.

$$\frac{3 \text{ ft}}{18 \text{ in.}} = \frac{3 \cdot \boxed{}}{18 \text{ in.}} = \underline{\hspace{1.5cm}} = \underline{\hspace{1.5cm}} = \underline{\hspace{1cm}}$$

Example 2   *Use Ratios*

In the diagram, $AB:BC$ is $4:1$ and $AC = 30$. Find AB and BC.

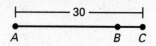

Solution

Let $x = BC$. Because the ratio of AB to BC is 4 to 1, you know $AB =$ ___ .

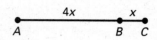

$AB + BC = AC$	Segment Addition Postulate
___ + ___ = ___	Substitute.
___ = ___	Add like terms.
$x =$ ___	Divide each side by ___ .

To find AB and BC, substitute your value for x.

$AB =$ ___ = ___ = ___ $BC = x =$ ___

Answer $AB =$ ___ and $BC =$ ___ .

Example 3   *Use Ratios*

The perimeter of a rectangle is 80 feet. The ratio of the length to the width is $7:3$. Find the length and the width.

Solution

The ratio of length to width is ___ to ___ , you can let the length $l =$ ___ and the width $w =$ ___ . Draw the rectangle at the right and label side lengths.

$2l + 2w = P$	Formula for perimeter of a rectangle
$2(\underline{\quad}) + 2(\underline{\quad}) = 80$	Substitute.
_____ = 80	Multiply.
___ = 80	Add like terms.
$x =$ ___	Divide each side by ___ .

To find length and width, substitute your value for x.

$l =$ ___ = ___ = ___ $w =$ ___ = ___ = ___

Answer The length is ___ feet and the width is ___ feet.

Follow-Up Check your answer for Example 3.

$2l + 2w = 2(\underline{}) + 2(\underline{}) = \underline{}$ $P = \underline{}$

● *Checkpoint* Complete the following exercises.

1. In the diagram, *EF* : *FG* is 2 : 1 and *EG* = 24. Find *EF* and *FG*.

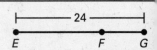

2. The perimeter of a rectangle is 84 feet. The ratio of the length to the width is 4 : 3. Find the length and the width of the rectangle.

CROSS PRODUCT PROPERTY

Words In a proportion, the product of the extremes is equal to the product of the

_____.

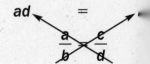

Symbols If $\dfrac{a}{b} = \dfrac{c}{d}$, then $\underline{} = \underline{}$.

Example 4   *Solve a Proportion*

Solve the proportion $\dfrac{5}{3} = \dfrac{y+2}{6}$.

Solution

$\dfrac{5}{3} = \dfrac{y+2}{6}$ **Write the original proportion.**

$(5)(\underline{}) = (3)(\underline{})$ **Cross product property**

$\underline{} = \underline{}$ **Multiply and use distributive property.**

$\underline{} = \underline{}$ **Subtract** ___ **from each side.**

$\underline{} = \underline{}$ **Divide each side by** ___.

✔ *Checkpoint* **Solve the proportion.**

3. $\dfrac{3}{x} = \dfrac{6}{8}$	4. $\dfrac{5}{3} = \dfrac{15}{y}$	5. $\dfrac{m+2}{5} = \dfrac{14}{10}$

7.2 Similar Polygons

Goal Identify similar polygons.

VOCABULARY

Similar polygons

Scale factor

Example 1 **Use Similarity Statements**

$\triangle PRQ$ and $\triangle STU$ are similar.

a. List all pairs of congruent angles.

b. Write the ratios of the corresponding sides in a statement of proportionality.

c. Check that the ratios of corresponding sides are equal.

Solution

a. $\angle P \cong \angle\underline{\quad}$, $\angle R \cong \angle\underline{\quad}$, $\angle Q \cong \angle\underline{\quad}$

b. $\dfrac{ST}{PR} = \underline{\quad\quad} = \underline{\quad\quad}$

c. Write the ratios of corresponding sides and simplify.

$\dfrac{ST}{PR} = \underline{\quad\quad}$, $\dfrac{TU}{RQ} = \underline{\quad\quad}$, $\dfrac{US}{QP} = \underline{\quad\quad}$

The ratios of corresponding sides are all equal to $\underline{\quad}$.

Example 2 | *Determine Whether Polygons are Similar*

Determine whether the triangles are similar. If they are similar, write a similarity statement and find the scale factor of Figure B to Figure A.

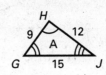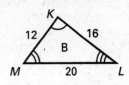

Solution

1. Check whether corresponding angles are congruent.

   From the diagram, $\angle G \cong \angle$___ , $\angle H \cong \angle$___ , and $\angle J \cong \angle$___ .
   So, the corresponding angles are _____ .

2. Check whether corresponding side lengths are proportional.

   $\dfrac{MK}{GH} =$ _____ , $\dfrac{KL}{HJ} =$ _____ , $\dfrac{LM}{JG} =$ _____

   All three ratios are equal, so the corresponding side lengths are

   _____ .

Answer By definition, the triangles are _____ . $\triangle GHJ \sim \triangle$ _____ .

The scale factor of Figure B to Figure A is ___ .

✔ **Checkpoint** Determine whether the polygons are similar.
If they are similar, write a similarity statement and find the
scale factor of Figure B to Figure A.

1.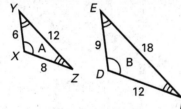

Example 3 Use Similar Polygons

△RST is similar to △GHJ. Find the value of x.

Solution

Because the triangles are similar, corresponding side lengths are proportional.

$$\frac{GH}{RS} = \underline{\quad\quad}$$ Write a proportion.

$$\underline{\quad\quad} = \underline{\quad\quad}$$ Substitute.

$$\underline{\quad\quad\quad} = \underline{\quad\quad\quad}$$ Cross product property

$$\underline{\quad\quad} = \underline{\quad\quad}$$ Multiply.

$$x = \underline{\quad\quad}$$ Divide each side by ___.

Example 4 Perimeters of Similar Polygons

A pool and the patio around the pool are similar rectangles.

a. Find the ratio of the length of the patio to the length of the pool.

b. Find the ratio of the perimeter of the patio to the perimeter of the pool.

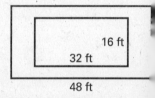

Solution

a. The ratio of the length of the patio to the length of the pool is

$$\frac{\text{length of patio}}{\text{length of pool}} = \underline{\quad\quad\quad} = \underline{\quad\quad}.$$

b. Perimeter of patio = _____ = _____ feet

Perimeter of pool = _____ = ___ feet

The ratio of the perimeter of the patio to the perimeter of the

pool is $\dfrac{\text{perimeter of patio}}{\text{perimeter of pool}} = \underline{\quad\quad\quad} = \underline{\quad\quad}.$

Follow-Up

In Example 4, what do you notice about the ratio of the lengths and the ratio of the perimeters?

THEOREM 7.1: PERIMETERS OF SIMILAR POLYGONS

Words If two polygons are similar, then the ratio of their perimeters is equal to the ratio of their corresponding _____.

Symbols If $\triangle ABC \sim \triangle DEF$, then

$$\frac{DE + EF + FD}{AB + BC + CA} = \frac{DE}{AB} = \frac{}{} = \frac{}{}.$$

✔ *Checkpoint* In the diagram, $\triangle PQR \sim \triangle STU$.

2. Find the value of x.

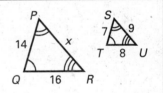

3. Find the ratio of the perimeter of $\triangle STU$ to the perimeter of $\triangle PQR$.

7.3 Showing Triangles are Similar: AA

Goal Show that two triangles are similar using the AA Similarity Postulate.

POSTULATE 15: ANGLE-ANGLE SIMILARITY POSTULATE (AA)

Words If two angles of one triangle are congruent to two angles of another triangle, then the two triangles are _____.

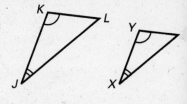

Symbols If $\angle K \cong \angle Y$ and $\angle J \cong \angle X$, then $\triangle JKL \sim \triangle XYZ$.

Example 1   Use the AA Similarity Postulate

Determine whether the triangles are similar. If they are similar, write a similarity statement. Explain.

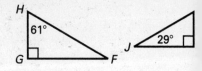

Solution

Look for two pairs of congruent angles.

1. $\angle G \cong \angle L$ because they are both _____.

2. Find $m\angle F$ to determine whether $\angle F$ is congruent to $\angle J$.

$m\angle F +$ ____ $+$ ____ $=$ ____   Triangle Sum Theorem

$m\angle F +$ ____ $=$ ____   Add.

$m\angle F =$ ____   Subtract ____ from each side.

Both $\angle F$ and $\angle J$ measure ____, so $\angle F$ ___ $\angle J$.

Answer By the AA Similarity Postulate, $\triangle$____ $\sim \triangle$____.

Example 2 **Use the AA Similarity Postulate**

Are you given enough information to
determine whether △*RST* is similar to
△*RUV*? Explain your reasoning.

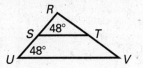

Solution

Redraw the diagram as two triangles: △*RUV* and △*RST*.

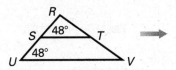

From the diagram, you know that both ∠*RST* and ∠_____
measure 48°, so ∠*RST* ≅ ∠_____.

Also, ∠*R* ≅ ∠*R* by the _____.

By the AA Similarity Postulate, △_____ ~ △_____.

✔ **Checkpoint** **Determine whether the triangles are similar. If
they are similar, write a similarity statement.**

1.

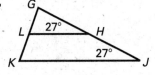

2.

Example 3 **Use Similar Triangles**

Find the value of x.

Solution

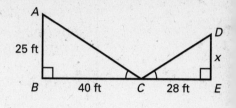

From the diagram, you know that
$\angle B \cong \angle$ _____ and $\angle ACB \cong \angle$ _____.
Therefore, $\triangle ABC \sim \triangle$ _____ by
the AA Similarity Postulate.

$\dfrac{DE}{AB} = $ _____   Write a proportion.

_____ = _____   Substitute.

_____ = _____   Cross product property

_____ = _____   Multiply.

$x = $ _____   Divide each side by _____.

Follow-Up

In Example 3, why do you need to show that the triangles are similar?

✔ **Checkpoint** Write a similarity statement for the triangles. The
find the value of the variable.

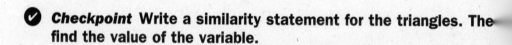

3.

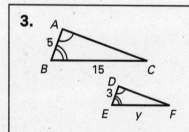

7.4 Showing Triangles are Similar: SSS and SAS

Goal Show that two triangles are similar using the SSS and SAS Similarity Theorems.

THEOREM 7.2: SIDE-SIDE-SIDE SIMILARITY THEOREM (SSS)

Words If the corresponding sides of two triangles are proportional, then the triangles are _____ .

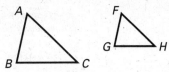

Symbols If $\dfrac{FG}{AB} = \dfrac{GH}{BC} = \dfrac{HF}{CA}$, then _____ .

Example 1 *Use the SSS Similarity Theorem*

Determine whether the triangles are similar. If they are similar, write a similarity statement and find the scale factor of Triangle B to Triangle A.

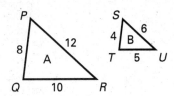

Solution

Write the ratios of corresponding sides and simplify.

$$\frac{SU}{PR} = \underline{\quad} = \underline{\quad}, \quad \frac{UT}{RQ} = \underline{\quad} = \underline{\quad}, \quad \frac{TS}{QP} = \underline{\quad} = \underline{\quad}$$

All three ratios are _____ . So, the corresponding sides of the triangle are _____ .

Answer By the SSS Similarity Theorem, _____ . The scale factor of Triangle B to Triangle A is ____ .

In Example 1, what is the scale factor of Triangle A to Triangle B?

Example 2   *Use the SSS Similarity Theorem*

Is either △DEF or △GHJ similar to △ABC?

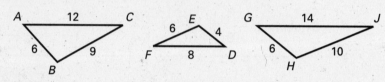

Solution

Look at the ratios of corresponding sides in △ABC and △DEF.

Shortest sides	Longest sides	Remaining sides
$\dfrac{DE}{AB} = \underline{\hspace{1cm}} = \underline{\hspace{1cm}}$	$\dfrac{FD}{CA} = \underline{\hspace{1cm}} = \underline{\hspace{1cm}}$	$\dfrac{EF}{BC} = \underline{\hspace{1cm}} = \underline{\hspace{1cm}}$

Answer Because all of the ratios _____, △ABC ~ _____.

Look at the ratios of corresponding sides in △ABC and △GHJ.

Shortest sides	Longest sides	Remaining sides
$\underline{\hspace{1cm}} = \underline{\hspace{1cm}} = \underline{\hspace{1cm}}$	$\underline{\hspace{1cm}} = \underline{\hspace{1cm}} = \underline{\hspace{1cm}}$	$\underline{\hspace{1cm}} = \underline{\hspace{1cm}}$

Answer Because the ratios _____, △ABC and △GHJ _____.

✓ Checkpoint Determine whether the triangles are similar. If they are similar, write a similarity statement.

1.

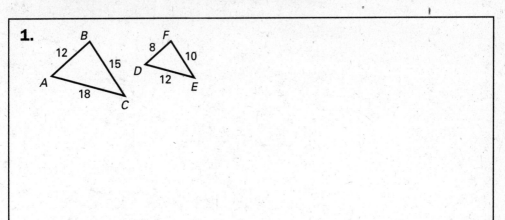

THEOREM 7.3: SIDE-ANGLE-SIDE SIMILARITY THEOREM (SAS)

Words If an angle of one triangle is congruent to an angle of a second triangle and the lengths of the sides that include these angles are proportional, then the triangles are _____.

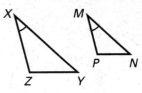

Symbols If $\angle X \cong$ _____ and $\dfrac{PM}{ZX} =$ _____ , then $\triangle XYZ \sim \triangle MNP$.

Example 3   *Use the SAS Similarity Theorem*

Determine whether the triangles are similar. If they are similar, write a similarity statement.

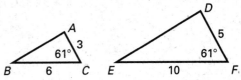

Solution

$\angle C$ and $\angle F$ both measure 61°, so _____.

Compare the ratios of the side lengths that include $\angle C$ and $\angle F$.

Shorter sides   =   Longer sides   =   =

_____ __   _____ __

The lengths of the sides that include $\angle C$ and $\angle F$ ____

_____.

Answer By the SAS Similarity Theorem, _____.

Example 4 **Similarity in Overlapping Triangles**

Show that △VYZ ~ △VWX.

Solution

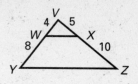

Draw △VYZ and △VWX separately.
Label the vertices and the side lengths.

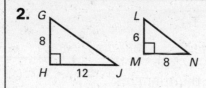 ⟶

∠V ≅ ∠V by the _____.

Shorter sides   =   =

_____ _____ _____

Longer sides   =   =

_____ _____ _____

The lengths of the sides that include ∠V _____.

Answer By the SAS Similarity Theorem, △VYZ ~ _____.

✓ **Checkpoint** Determine whether the triangles are similar. If the
are similar, write a similarity statement. Explain.

2.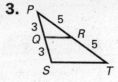

3.

Proportions and Similar Triangles

Goal Use the Triangle Proportionality Theorem and its converse.

VOCABULARY

Midsegment of a triangle

THEOREM 7.4: TRIANGLE PROPORTIONALITY THEOREM

Words If a line parallel to one side of a triangle intersects the other two sides, then it divides the two sides _____.

Symbols In $\triangle QRS$, if $\overline{TU} \parallel \overline{QS}$ then $\dfrac{RT}{TQ} = $ ____.

Example 1 *Find Segment Lengths*

Find the value of x.

Solution

$\dfrac{CD}{DB} = $ ____   Triangle Proportionality Theorem

___ = ___ ___   Substitute.

_____ = _____   Cross product property

___ = ___   Multiply.

___ $= x$ Divide each side by ___.

Example 2 *Find Segment Lengths*

Find the value of *y*.

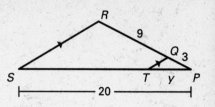

Solution

You know that *PS* = 20 and
PT = *y*. By the Segment Addition
Postulate, *TS* = 20 − *y*.

$\dfrac{PQ}{QR} = \underline{\hspace{1.5cm}}$ **Triangle Proportionality Theorem**

$\underline{\hspace{1cm}} = \dfrac{\underline{\hspace{1cm}}}{\underline{\hspace{1cm}}}$ **Substitute.**

$\dfrac{\underline{\hspace{2cm}}}{} = \underline{\hspace{1cm}}$ **Cross product property**

$\dfrac{\underline{\hspace{2cm}}}{} = \underline{\hspace{1cm}}$ **Distributive property**

$\underline{\hspace{1cm}} = \underline{\hspace{1cm}}$ **Add ___ to each side.**

$\underline{\hspace{1cm}} = y$ **Divide each side by ___.**

Follow-Up

In Example 2, what is *TS*?

THEOREM 7.5: CONVERSE OF TRIANGLE PROPORTIONALITY THEOREM

Words If a line divides two sides of a
triangle proportionally, then it is _____
to the third side.

Symbols In △*QRS*, if $\dfrac{RT}{TQ} = \dfrac{RU}{US}$,

then $\overline{TU} \parallel$ ___ .

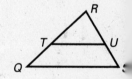

Example 3 **Determine Parallels**

Given the diagram, determine whether $\overline{MN}$ is parallel to $\overline{GH}$.

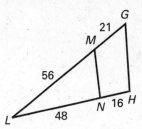

Solution

Find and simplify the ratios of the two sides divided by $\overline{MN}$.

$$\frac{\quad}{\quad} = \frac{\quad}{\quad} = \frac{\quad}{\quad} \qquad\qquad \frac{\quad}{\quad} = \frac{\quad}{\quad} = \frac{\quad}{\quad}$$

Answer Because _____ , $\overline{MN}$ _____ to $\overline{GH}$.

✔ **Checkpoint** Find the value of the variable.

1. 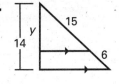	**2.**

Given the diagram, determine whether $\overline{QR}$ is parallel to $\overline{ST}$. Explain.

3. 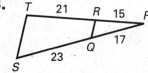	**4.** 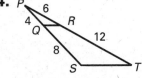

THEOREM 7.6: THE MIDSEGMENT THEOREM

Words The segment connecting the midpoints of two sides of a triangle is _____ to the third side and is _____ as long.

Symbols In $\triangle ABC$, if $CD = DA$ and $CE = EB$, then $\overline{DE} \parallel$ _____ and $DE =$ _____ .

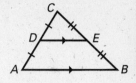

Follow-Up

What is the relationship between Theorems 7.4 and 7.6?

Example 4   *Use the Midsegment Theorem*

Given the diagram, find the length of $\overline{QS}$.

Solution
From the marks on the diagram, you know that S is the midpoint of _____ and Q is the midpoint of _____ . So, $\overline{QS}$ is a _____ of $\triangle PRT$.

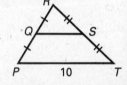

Use the Midsegment Theorem. $QS =$ _____ $=$ _____ $=$ __

Answer The length of $\overline{QS}$ is __ .

✔ **Checkpoint** Find the value of the variable.

5.

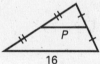

16

6.

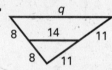

7.6 Dilations

Goal Identify and draw dilations.

VOCABULARY

Dilation

Reduction

Enlargement

Example 1 *Identify Dilations*

Tell whether the dilation is a *reduction* or an *enlargement*.

a.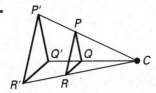

b.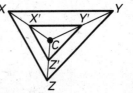

Solution

a. The dilation is an enlargement because the image
   ($\triangle P'Q'R'$) is larger than the original figure ($\triangle PQR$).

b. The dilation is a reduction because the image ($\triangle X'Y'Z'$)
   is smaller than the original figure ($\triangle XYZ$).

Example 2   *Find Scale Factors*

Find the scale factor of the dilation.

a.

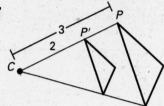

b.

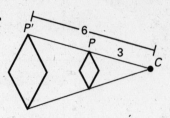

Solution

Find the ratio of *CP'* to *CP*.

a. scale factor $= \dfrac{CP'}{CP} = $ ____

b. scale factor $= \dfrac{CP'}{CP} = $ ____ $=$

Follow-Up In Example 2, tell whether the dilation is a *reduction* o——
enlargement. Give two ways to support your answer.

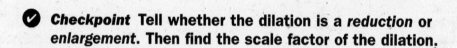

a.

b.

✔ **Checkpoint** Tell whether the dilation is a *reduction* or *enlargement*. Then find the scale factor of the dilation.

1.

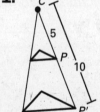

2.

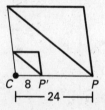

Example 3 **Dilations and Similar Figures**

△P'Q'R' is the image of △PQR after a reduction. Find the value of x.

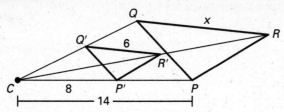

Solution

$$\frac{CP'}{CP} = \underline{\hspace{2cm}}$$ Write a proportion.

$$\underline{\hspace{1cm}} = \frac{\underline{\hspace{0.5cm}}}{\underline{\hspace{0.5cm}}}$$ Substitute.

$$\underline{\hspace{2cm}} = \underline{\hspace{2cm}}$$ Cross product property

$$\underline{\hspace{1cm}} = \underline{\hspace{0.5cm}}$$ Multiply.

$$x = \underline{\hspace{1.5cm}}$$ Divide each side by __ .

✔ **Checkpoint** Find the value of the variable.

3.

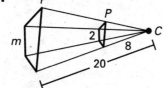

4.

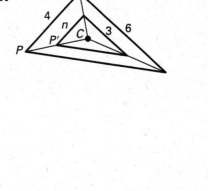

Words to Review

Give an example of the vocabulary word.

Ratio	Proportion
Extremes	Means
Similar polygons	Scale factor
Midsegment of a triangle	Dilation

Reduction	Enlargement

Review your notes and Chapter 7 by using the Chapter Summary and Review on pages 400–403 of your textbook.

8.1 Classifying Polygons

Goal Describe polygons.

VOCABULARY

Convex

Concave

Equilateral

Equiangular

Regular

Example 1 *Identify Convex and Concave Polygons*

Decide whether the polygon is *convex* or *concave*.

a.

b.

Solution

Draw the extended sides. Does any extended side pass through th
interior of the polygon?

a. The polygon is _____ because _____
   passes through the interior of the polygon.

b. The polygon is _____ because _____
   pass through the interior of the polygon.

Follow-Up Tell whether the statement is *true* or *false*.

All triangles are convex. _____

All triangles are concave. _____

A triangle can be either convex or concave. _____

Draw a line to match the description with the name.

equilateral, but not equiangular   square

equiangular, but not equilateral   rectangle

regular   rhombus

Example 2   *Identify Regular Polygons*

Decide whether the polygon is regular. Explain your answer.

a.   b.   c.

Solution

a. Is the polygon: equilateral? _____
                   equiangular? _____
                   both equilateral and equiangular? _____
                   regular? _____

b. Is the polygon: equilateral? _____
                   equiangular? _____
                   both equilateral and equiangular? _____
                   regular? _____

c. Is the polygon: equilateral? _____
                   equiangular? _____
                   both equilateral and equiangular? _____
                   regular? _____

Follow-Up Draw the polygon described.

equilateral but not equiangular	equiangular but not equilateral	convex and regular	convex but not regular

Tell whether the statement is *true* or *false*.

Any equilateral triangle is also regular. _____

Any equiangular triangle is also regular. _____

✓ **Checkpoint** Decide whether the polygon is *convex* or *concav*
Then decide whether the polygon is regular. Explain your
answer.

1.	2.	3.

8.2 Angles in Polygons

Goal Find the measures of interior and exterior angles of polygons.

THEOREM 8.1: POLYGON INTERIOR ANGLES THEOREM

Words The sum of the measures of the interior angles of a convex polygon with n sides is

_____ .

$n = 6$

Symbols $m\angle 1 + m\angle 2 + \ldots + m\angle n =$ _____

Follow-Up

The Triangle Sum Theorem states that the sum of the measures of the angles of a triangle is ____°. To use Theorem 8.1 with a triangle, substitute ___ for n.

$(n - 2) \cdot 180° = (\_\_ - 2) \cdot 180° = \_\_ \cdot 180° = \_\_\_°$ ✓

The Quadrilateral Interior Angles Theorem states that the sum of the measures of the interior angles of a quadrilateral is ____°. To use Theorem 8.1 with a quadrilateral, substitute ___ for n.

$(n - 2) \cdot 180° = (\_\_ - 2) \cdot 180° = \_\_ \cdot 180° = \_\_\_°$ ✓

Example 1 *Use the Polygon Interior Angles Theorem*

Find the sum of the measures of the interior angles of the convex heptagon shown.

Solution

A heptagon has ___ sides. Use the Polygon Interior Angles Theorem and substitute ___ for n.

$(n - 2) \cdot 180° = (\_\_ - 2) \cdot 180° = \_\_ \cdot 180° = \_\_\_°$

Answer The sum of the measures of the interior angles of the convex heptagon is ____°.

Follow-Up

In Example 1, is your answer true for *any* convex heptagon?

Example 2 *Find the Measure of an Interior Angle*

Find the measure of ∠A in the diagram.

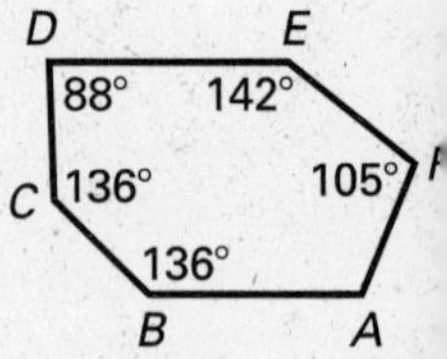

Diagram labels: D, E, 88°, 142°, C, 136°, 105° F, 136°, B, A

Solution

The polygon has ___ sides. Use the Polygon
Interior Angles Theorem and substitute ___ for *n*.

$(n - 2) \cdot 180° = (\underline{} - 2) \cdot 180° = \underline{} \cdot 180° = \underline{}°$

Use your answer to write an equation for the sum of the measures
of the interior angles. Solve for *m∠A*.

$m∠A + m∠B + m∠C + m∠D + m∠E + m∠F = \underline{}°$

$m∠A + \underline{}° + \underline{}° + \underline{}° + \underline{}° + \underline{}° = \underline{}°$

$m∠A + \underline{}° = \underline{}°$

$m∠A = \underline{}°$

Example 3 *Interior Angles of a Regular Polygon*

Find the measure of an interior angle of a
regular octagon.

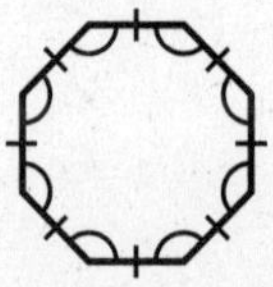

Solution

An octagon has ___ sides. Use the Polygon
Interior Angles Theorem and substitute ___ for *n*.

$(n - 2) \cdot 180° = (\underline{} - 2) \cdot 180° = \underline{} \cdot 180° = \underline{}°$

Because the octagon is regular, each angle has the same measur⟩
So, divide to find the measure of one interior angle.

$\underline{}° \div \underline{} = \underline{}°$

Answer The measure of an interior angle of a regular octagon
is ___°.

Follow-Up Complete the table for a regular *n*-gon.

n	3	4	5	6	7	8	9
Sum of the measures of the interior angles							
Measure of one interior angle							

✓ **Checkpoint** In Exercises 1–3, find the measure of ∠G.

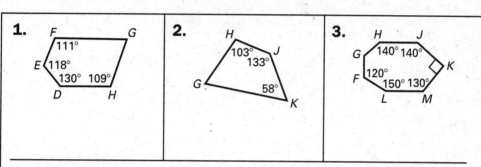

1. F, G, E 118°, F 111°, D 130°, H 109°

2. H 103°, J 133°, G, 58°, K

3. H, J, G 140° 140°, K, F 120°, L 150° 130° M

4. Find the measure of an interior angle of a regular polygon with twelve sides.

THEOREM 8.2: POLYGON EXTERIOR ANGLES THEOREM

Words The sum of the measures of the exterior angles of a convex polygon, one angle at each vertex, is ____°.

Symbols $m\angle 1 + m\angle 2 + \ldots + m\angle n =$ ____°

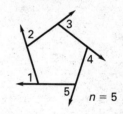

n = 5

Example 4   *Find the Measure of an Exterior Angle*

Find the value of *x*.

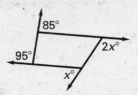

Solution

Using the Polygon Exterior Angles Theorem, set the sum of the measures of the exterior angles equal to ____°.

$95° + 85° + 2x° + x° = $ ____ °   **Polygon Exterior Angles Theorem**

      ____ $+$ ____ $=$ ____   **Combine like terms.**

           ____ $=$ ____   **Subtract** ____ **from each side.**

           __ $=$ __   **Divide each side by** __ .

Answer The value of *x* is ____ .

Follow-Up Check your answer for Example 4.

$95° + 85° + x° + 2x° = 95° + 85° + $ ____ ° $+ 2($ ____ $)° = $ ____ ° ✓

✓ **Checkpoint** Find the value of *x*.

5.

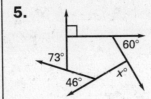

6.

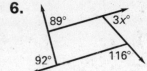

8.3 Area of Squares and Rectangles

Goal Find the area of squares and rectangles.

VOCABULARY

Area

AREA OF A SQUARE

Words The area of a square is the square of the length of its _____.

Symbols $A = \underline{\quad}^2$

Example 1 *Find the Area of a Square*

Find the area of the square.

Solution

Use the formula for the area of a square and substitute ___ for *s*.

$$A = s^2 = (\underline{\quad})^2 = \underline{\quad}$$

Answer The area of the square is ___ square feet.

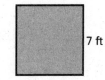

7 ft

Follow-Up

Suppose you know that the area of a square is 49 square feet. What calculation can you perform to find the length of a side of the square?

AREA OF A RECTANGLE

Words The area of a rectangle is the
product of its _____ and _____.

Symbols $A = bh$

Example 2 *Find the Area of a Rectangle*

Find the area of the rectangle.

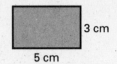

3 cm

5 cm

Solution

Use the formula for the area of a rectangle.
Substitute ___ for b and ___ for h.

$A = bh = (\_\_)(\_\_) = \_\_\_$

Answer The area of the rectangle is ___ square centimeters.

Follow-Up

Find the area of the figure at the right
using the formula for the area of a
square.

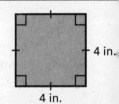

4 in.

4 in.

$A = \_\_^2 = \_\_^2 = \_\_\_$ square inches

Find the area of the figure above using the formula for the area
of a rectangle.

$A = \_\_\_ = \_\_ \cdot \_\_ = \_\_\_$ square inches

Why can you use either formula to find the area?

Example 3 *Find the Height of a Rectangle*

The rectangle has an area
of 54 square inches. Find
its height.

$A = 54$ in.^{2} h

9 in.

Solution

$A = \underline{}h$ **Formula for the area of a rectangle**

$\underline{} = (\underline{}) \cdot h$ **Substitute** $\underline{}$ **for** A **and** $\underline{}$ **for** b.

$\underline{} = h$ **Divide each side by** $\underline{}$.

Answer The height of the rectangle is _____ .

✓ **Checkpoint** Find the area of the quadrilateral.

1. 11 m	**2.** 2 ft 6 ft	**3.** 4.5 yd 5.9 yd

4. A rectangle has an area of 52 square meters and a height of 4 meters. Find the length of its base.

Example 4 *Divide a Complex Polygon into Rectangles*

Find the dimensions of rectangles A and B.

2   5
7   B   A
9

Solution

Rectangle A

The base is ___ units.

Because rectangle B is ___ units taller than
rectangle A, the height of rectangle A is ___ − ___ = ___ units.

Rectangle B

The height is ___ units.

The base of rectangle B is the total of both bases minus the base
of rectangle A, or ___ − ___ = ___ units.

Example 5   *Find the Area of a Complex Polygon*

Find the area of the polygon made
up of rectangles.

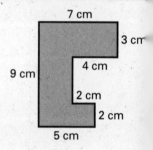

7 cm

3 cm

9 cm

4 cm

2 cm

2 cm

5 cm

Solution

Divide the polygon into three rectangles:
F, G, and H.

Area F = ___ • ___ = ___ cm²

Area G = ___ • ___ = ___ cm²

Area H = ___ • ___ = ___ cm²

    Total area = Area F + Area G + Area H

            = ___ + ___ + ___ = ___

Answer The area of the polygon is ___ square centimeters.

Follow-Up

In Example 5, divide the polygon into
different rectangles to find the area.
Label the diagram and show your work.

7 cm

3 cm

9 cm

4 cm

2 cm

2 cm

5 cm

✔ *Checkpoint* **Find the area of the polygon made up of
rectangles.**

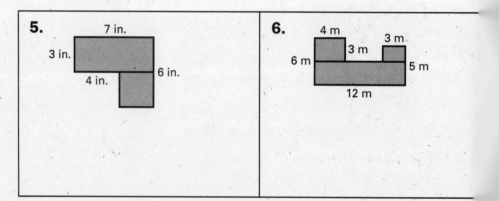

5.

7 in.

3 in.

4 in.

6 in.

6.

4 m

3 m

3 m

6 m

5 m

12 m

8.4 Area of Triangles

Find the area of triangles.

VOCABULARY

Height of a triangle, base of a triangle

AREA OF A TRIANGLE

Words The area of a triangle is
one half the product of a _____
and its corresponding _____ .

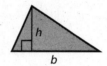

Symbols $A =$ _____

Follow-Up

Compare and contrast the formulas for the area of a triangle and
the area of a rectangle.

How are they alike?

How are they different?

Example 1   *Find the Area of a Right Triangle*

Find the area of the right triangle.

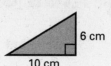

6 cm

10 cm

Solution

Use the formula for the area of a triangle.
Substitute ___ for b and ___ for h.

$$A = \frac{1}{2}bh = \frac{1}{2}(\underline{\quad})(\underline{\quad}) = \underline{\quad} \text{ square centimeters}$$

Example 2   *Find the Area of a Triangle*

Find the area of the triangle.

a.

5 ft

8 ft

b.

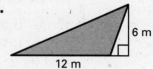

6 m

12 m

Solution

a. Use the formula for the area of a triangle and substitute ___ for b and ___ for h.

$$A = \frac{1}{2}bh = \frac{1}{2}(\underline{\quad})(\underline{\quad}) = \underline{\quad} \text{ square feet}$$

b. Use the formula for the area of a triangle and substitute ___ for b and ___ for h.

$$A = \frac{1}{2}bh = \frac{1}{2}(\underline{\quad})(\underline{\quad}) = \underline{\quad} \text{ square meters}$$

✓ *Checkpoint* **Find the area of the triangle.**

1.	2.	3.
8 in. 9 in.	7 yd 12 yd	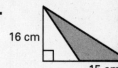 16 cm 15 cm

Example 3   *Find the Height of a Triangle*

Find the height of the triangle, given
that its area is 39 square inches.

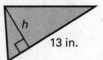

13 in.

Solution

$A = \frac{1}{2}bh$ Formula for the area of a triangle.

$\underline{} = \frac{1}{2}(\underline{}) \cdot h$ Substitute ___ for *A* and ___ for *b*.

$\underline{} = \underline{} h$ Multiply each side by ___.

$\underline{} = h$ Divide each side by ___.

Answer The height of the triangle is ___ inches.

Follow-Up

Complete the table at the right for a
triangle with area *A* square units,
base *b* units, and height *h* units.

A	b	h
21	7	
30		10
	8	4

✔ *Checkpoint* Find the missing measure.

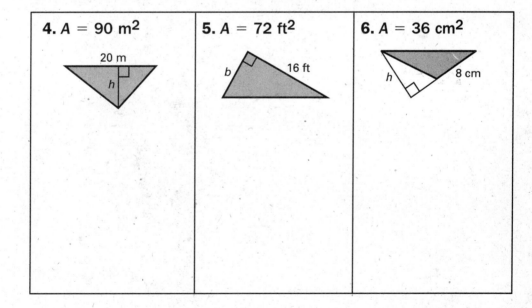

4. A = 90 m²

20 m

h

5. A = 72 ft²

b   16 ft

6. A = 36 cm²

h   8 cm

Example 4 *Areas of Similar Triangles*

a. Find the ratio of the areas of the similar triangles.

b. Find the scale factor of △*ABC* to △*DEF* and compare it to the ratio of their areas.

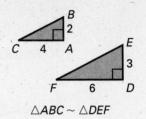

△*ABC* ~ △*DEF*

Solution

a. Area of △*ABC* = $\frac{1}{2}bh$ = $\frac{1}{2}$(__)(__) = ___ square units.

Area of △*DEF* = $\frac{1}{2}bh$ = $\frac{1}{2}$(__)(__) = ___ square units.

Ratio of areas = $\dfrac{\text{Area of } \triangle ABC}{\text{Area of } \triangle DEF}$ = ___.

b. The scale factor of △*ABC* to △*DEF* is ___.

The ratio of the areas is the _____ of the scale factor.

$$\frac{\boxed{}^2}{\boxed{}^2} = \underline{}$$

THEOREM 8.3: AREAS OF SIMILAR POLYGONS

Words If two polygons are similar with a scale factor of $\frac{a}{b}$, then the ratio of their areas is ___.

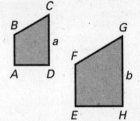

Symbols If *ABCD* ~ *EFGH* with a scale factor of $\frac{a}{b}$, then $\dfrac{\text{Area of } ABCD}{\text{Area of } EFGH}$ = ___.

8.5 Area of Parallelograms

Goal Find the area of parallelograms.

VOCABULARY

Base of a parallelogram

_____

Height of a parallelogram

AREA OF A PARALLELOGRAM

Words The area of a parallelogram
is the product of a _____ and its
corresponding _____.

Symbols $A = $ ____

Follow-Up

For each formula, draw a diagram and write the formula.

Area of a Rectangle   **Area of a Parallelogram**

_____

Compare the formulas.

Example 1 — Find the Area of a Parallelogram

Find the area of the parallelogram.

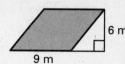

6 m

9 m

Solution

Use the formula for the area of a parallelogram.
Substitute ___ for *b* and ___ for *h*.

$A = bh = (\_\_)(\_\_) = \_\_$

Answer The parallelogram has an area of ____ square meters.

Example 2 — Find the Height of a Parallelogram

Find the height of the parallelogram,
given that its area is 78 square feet.

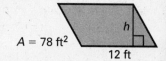

$A = 78\ \text{ft}^2$

h

12 ft

Solution

$A = bh$ Formula for the area of a parallelogram

$\_\_ = \_\_ h$ Substitute ____ for *A* and ____ for *b*.

$\_\_ = h$ Divide each side by ____.

Answer The height of the parallelogram is ____ feet.

✔ **Checkpoint** Find the area of the parallelogram.

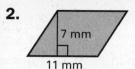

1.

12 yd

8 yd

2.

7 mm

11 mm

3.

14 ft

14 ft

In Exercises 4–6, *A* represents the area of the parallelogram.
Find the missing measure.

4. A = 72 in.²

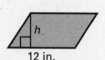

h

12 in.

5. A = 30 m²

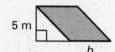

5 m

b

6. A = 28 cm²

h

7 cm

AREA OF A RHOMBUS

Words The area of a rhombus is equal to _____ the product of the lengths of the _____.

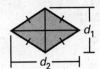

Symbols $A = $

_____

Example 3 *Find the Area of a Rhombus*

Find the area of the rhombus.

a.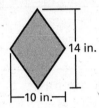

14 in.

10 in.

b.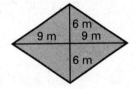

6 m
9 m   9 m
6 m

Solution

a. $A = \frac{1}{2}d_1d_2 = \frac{1}{2}(\underline{})(\underline{}) = \underline{}$ square inches

b. $A = \frac{1}{2}d_1d_2 = \frac{1}{2}(\underline{})(\underline{}) = \underline{}$ square meters

---

✔ **Checkpoint** Find the area of the rhombus.

7.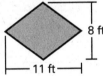

8 ft

11 ft

8.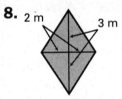

2 m   3 m

9.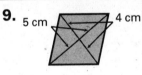

5 cm   4 cm

8.6 Area of Trapezoids

Goal Find the area of trapezoids.

VOCABULARY

Height of a trapezoid

Follow-Up

For each trapezoid below, label the bases b_1 and b_2. Then label (and draw if necessary) the height h.

Complete each statement with *always*, *sometimes*, or *never*.

The bases of a trapezoid are _____ parallel.

The bases of a trapezoid are _____ congruent.

The bases of a trapezoid are _____ sides of the trapezoid.

The height of a trapezoid is _____ a side of the trapezoid.

The height of a trapezoid is _____ perpendicular to both bases.

AREA OF A TRAPEZOID

Words The area of a trapezoid is one half the product of the _____ and the sum of the _____.

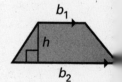

Symbols $A = $

_____

Example 1   *Find the Area of a Trapezoid*

Find the area of the trapezoid.

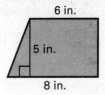

6 in.

5 in.

8 in.

Solution

$$A = \frac{1}{2}h(b_1 + b_2)$$ Formula for the area of a trapezoid

$$= \frac{1}{2}(\_\_)(\_\_ + \_\_)$$ Substitute ___ for *h*, ___ for b_1, and ___ for b_2.

$$= \frac{1}{2}(\_\_)(\_\_)$$ Simplify within parentheses.

$$= \_\_$$ Simplify.

Answer The area of the trapezoid is ___ square inches.

✔ *Checkpoint* Find the area of the trapezoid.

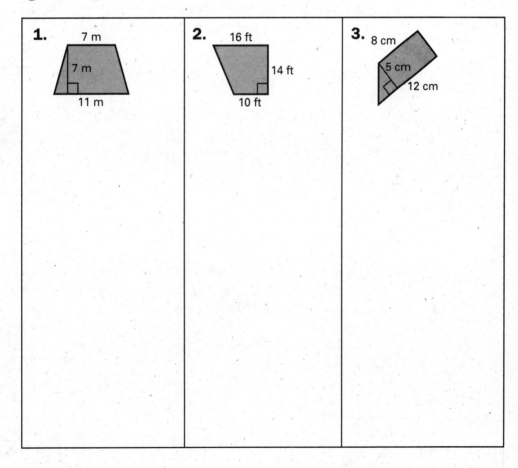

1.

7 m

7 m

11 m

2.

16 ft

14 ft

10 ft

3.

8 cm

5 cm

12 cm

Example 2   *Use the Area of a Trapezoid*

Find the value of b_2, given that the area of the trapezoid is 96 square meters.

9 m

8 m

$A = 96\ m^2$

b_2

Solution

$$A = \frac{1}{2}h(b_1 + b_2)$$ Formula for the area of a trapezoid

$$\underline{\quad} = \frac{1}{2}(\underline{\quad})(\underline{\quad} + b_2)$$ Substitute ____ for A, ___ for h, and ___ for b_1.

$$\underline{\quad} = (\underline{\quad})(\underline{\quad} + b_2)$$ Multiply each side by ___.

$$\underline{\quad} = \underline{\quad} + \underline{\quad}b_2$$ Use the _____ property.

$$\underline{\quad} = \underline{\quad}b_2$$ Subtract ____ from each side.

$$\underline{\quad} = b_2$$ Divide each side by ___.

Answer The value of b_2 is ___ meters.

✓ *Checkpoint* In Exercises 4–6, A gives the area of the trapezoid. Find the missing measure.

4. $A = 77\ ft^2$	5. $A = 39\ cm^2$	6. $A = 84\ in.^2$
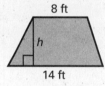 8 ft, h, 14 ft	b_1, 6 cm, 8 cm	13 in., 8 in, b_2

7. A trapezoid has an area of 294 square yards. Its height is 14 yards and the length of one base is 30 yards. Find the length of the other base.

Follow-Up Summarize the area formulas you have learned in this chapter. Write the formula, then draw and label a diagram.

Polygon	Area Formula	Diagram
Square		
Rectangle		
Triangle		
Parallelogram		
Rhombus		
Trapezoid		

8.7 Circumference and Area of Circles

Goal Find the circumference and area of circles.

VOCABULARY

Circle, center

Radius

Diameter

Circumference

Central angle

Sector

CIRCUMFERENCE OF A CIRCLE

Words The circumference of a circle is the product of ___ and the _____ or twice the product of ___ and the _____.

Symbols $C =$ ____ or $C =$ ____

Example 1 *Find the Circumference of a Circle*

Find the circumference of the circle.

4 in.

Solution

$C = 2\pi r$ Formula for circumference

$= 2\pi(\underline{\ \ })$ Subtitute ___ for *r*.

$= \underline{\ \ }\pi$ Simplify.

$\approx \underline{\ \ }(\underline{\ \ \ \ })$ Use _____ as an approximation for π.

$= \underline{\ \ \ \ \ }$ Multiply.

Answer The circumference is about ___ inches.

✓ **Checkpoint** Find the circumference of the circle. Round your answer to the nearest whole number.

1. 6 cm	2. 9 ft	3. 16 in.

AREA OF A CIRCLE

Words The area of a circle is the product of ___ and _____.

Symbols $A =$ _____

Example 2   *Find the Area of a Circle*

Find the area of the circle.

7 cm

Solution

$A = \pi r^2$ **Formula for area of a circle**

$ = \pi(\underline{})^2$ **Substitute ___ for r.**

$ = (\underline{})\pi$ **Simplify.**

$ \approx \underline{}$ **Use a calculator.**

Answer The area is about _____ square centimeters.

Example 3   *Use the Area of a Circle*

Find the radius of a circle with an area
of 380 square feet.

Solution

$A = 380 \text{ ft}^2$

$A = \pi r^2$ **Formula for area of a circle**

$\underline{} = \pi r^2$ **Substitute the _____ for A.**

$\underline{} \approx r^2$ **Divide each side by ___. Use a calculator.**

$\underline{} \approx r$ **Take the _____.**

Answer The radius is about ___ feet.

✓ *Checkpoint* In Exercises 4–6, find the area of the circle. Rou
your answer to the nearest whole number.

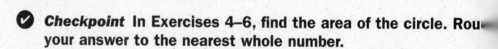

4.

8 in.

5.

3 cm

6.

12 ft

7. Find the radius of a circle with an area of 113 square meters.

Example 4 *Find the Area of a Sector*

Find the area of the shaded sector.

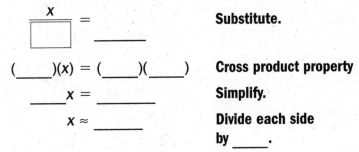

Solution

1. Find the area of the circle.

$$A = \pi r^2 = \pi(\underline{})^2 \approx \underline{} \text{ square meters}$$

2. Find the area of the sector. Let ___ be the area of the sector.

$$\frac{\text{Area of sector}}{\text{Area of entire circle}} = \frac{\text{Measure of central angle}}{\text{Measure of entire circle}}$$

$$\frac{x}{\boxed{}} = \underline{} \qquad \text{Substitute.}$$

$$(\underline{})(x) = (\underline{})(\underline{}) \qquad \text{Cross product property}$$

$$\underline{}\,x = \underline{} \qquad \text{Simplify.}$$

$$x \approx \underline{} \qquad \text{Divide each side by } \underline{}.$$

Answer The area of the sector is about ____ square meters.

✔ **Checkpoint** In Exercises 8 and 9, *A* represents the area of the entire circle and *x* represents the area of the shaded sector. Complete the proportion used to find the value of *x*. Do not solve the proportion.

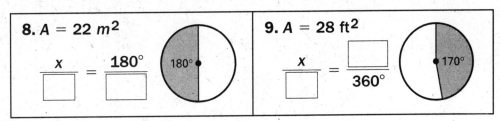

8. $A = 22 \text{ m}^2$

$$\frac{x}{\boxed{}} = \frac{180°}{\boxed{}}$$

9. $A = 28 \text{ ft}^2$

$$\frac{x}{\boxed{}} = \frac{\boxed{}}{360°}$$

Find the area of the shaded sector. Round your answer to the nearest whole number.

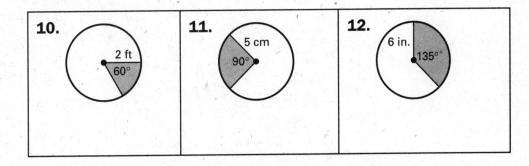

10.

11.

12.

Words to Review

Give an example of the vocabulary word.

Convex	Concave
Equilateral	Equiangular
Regular	Area
Height, base of a triangle	Height, base of a parallelogram

Height of a trapezoid	Circle
Center, radius, diameter of circle	Circumference
Central angle	Sector

Review your notes and Chapter 8 by using the Chapter Summary and Review on pages 460–463 of your textbook.

9.1 Solid Figures

Goal Identify and name solid figures.

VOCABULARY

Solid

_____

Polyhedron, face, edge

Example 1 *Identify and Name Polyhedra*

Tell whether the solid is a polyhedron. Describe the shape of the base and then name the solid.

a.

b.

Solution

a. The solid is formed by _____, so it ___ a polyhedron. The bases are congruent _____ in parallel planes. This figure i
   a _____.

b. A cylinder has a _____ surface, so it _____ a polyhedron.

Example 2   Find Faces and Edges

Use the diagram at the right.

a. Name the polyhedron.

b. Count the number of faces and edges.

c. List any congruent faces and edges.

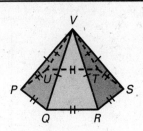

Solution

a. The solid has _____ base(s). The shape of the base(s) is a
_____ . So, the polyhedron is a _____ .

b. The polyhedron has ___ faces and ___ edges.

c. Congruent faces

_____ ≅ _____ ≅ _____ ≅ _____ ≅ _____ ≅ _____

Congruent edges

$\overline{PQ} \cong \overline{QR} \cong \overline{RS} \cong \overline{ST} \cong \overline{TU} \cong \overline{UP}$

$\overline{PV} \cong \overline{QV} \cong \overline{RV} \cong \overline{SV} \cong \overline{TV} \cong \overline{UV}$

Example 3   Sketch a Polyhedron

Sketch a triangular prism.

Solution

Use the space at the right, and follow these steps.

1. Draw two congruent triangular bases.

2. Connect corresponding vertices of the bases with vertical lines.

3. Partially erase the hidden lines to create dashed lines. Shade the prism.

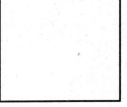

Follow-Up Sketch each solid below.

Prisms		
Rectangular Prism	Triangular Prism	Cube

Pyramids		
Rectangular Pyramid	Triangular Pyramid	Pentagonal Pyramid
Cylinder	Cone	Sphere

✓ **Checkpoint** Tell whether the solid is a polyhedron. If so, identify the shape of the base(s). Then name the solid.

1.	2.	3.

Surface Area of Prisms and Cylinders

Goal Find the surface areas of prisms and cylinders.

VOCABULARY

Prism

Lateral face

Surface area

Lateral area

Cylinder

SURFACE AREA OF A PRISM

Words The surface area of a prism is the sum of twice the area of a _____ and the product of the _____ of the base and the _____.

Symbols $S = 2\_\_ + \_\_\_ = 2(\_\_\_) + (\_\_ + \_\_\_)(\_\_)$

Example 1   Use the Net of a Prism

Find the surface area of
the rectangular prism.

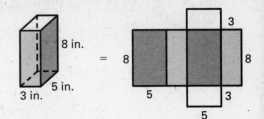

Solution

Find the areas of all the rectangles that are faces of the prism.

Congruent Faces	Dimensions	Area of Face
Left and _____ faces	_____ by _____	
Front and _____ faces	_____ by _____	
Top and _____ faces	_____ by _____	

Add the areas to find the surface area.

$$S = 2(\underline{}) + 2(\underline{}) + 2(\underline{}) = \underline{}$$

Answer The surface area is _____.

Example 2   Find Surface Area of a Prism

Find the surface area of the prism.

Solution

1. Find the area of a base.

$$B = \frac{1}{2}bh = \frac{1}{2} \cdot \underline{} \cdot \underline{} = \underline{} \text{ m}^2$$

2. Find the perimeter of a base.

$$P = \underline{} + \underline{} + \underline{} = \underline{} \text{ m}$$

3. Find the height of the prism.

$$h = \underline{} \text{ m}$$

4. Use the Surface Area of a Prism formula.

$$S = 2B + Ph = 2(\underline{}) + (\underline{})(\underline{}) = \underline{}$$

Answer The surface area of the prism is _____.

✔ **Checkpoint** Find the surface area of the prism.

1. 3 in. / 6 in. / 2 in.	**2.** 6 ft / 8 ft / 5 ft	**3.** 8 cm / 6 cm / 4 cm / 10 cm

SURFACE AREA OF A CYLINDER

Words The surface area of a cylinder is
the sum of twice the area of a _____ and
the product of the _____ of the
base and the _____.

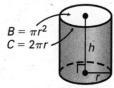

$B = \pi r^2$
$C = 2\pi r$

h

r

Symbols $S = 2\_\_ + \_\_ = 2(\_\_) + (\_\_)(\_\_)$

Example 3 *Find Surface Area of a Cylinder*

Find the surface area of the cylinder.
Round your answer to the nearest
whole number.

4 ft

3 ft

Solution

The radius of the base is ___ feet and the height is ___ feet. Use
these values in the formula for surface area of a cylinder.

$S = 2\pi r^2 + 2\pi rh$ Formula for _____

$= 2\pi(\_\_)^2 + 2\pi(\_\_)(\_\_)$ Substitute ___ for r and ___ for h.

$= \_\_ \pi + \_\_ \pi$ Simplify.

$= \_\_ \pi$ Add.

$\approx \_\_\_$ Multiply.

Answer The surface area is about _____.

Example 4 Find Lateral Area

About how much plastic is used to make a straw that has a diameter of 5 millimeters and a height of 195 millimeters?

Solution

The straw is a _____ with no _____. Use the formula for the surface area of a cylinder, but do not include _____ _____.

The diameter is 5 mm. So the radius is 5 ÷ 2 = 2.5 mm.

Lateral area = 2πrh		Surface area formula without _____.
= 2π(____)(____)		Substitute values.
= ____ π		Simplify.
≈ 3063		Multiply.

Answer About _____ of plastic is used.

✔ **Checkpoint** Find the area described. Round your answer to th nearest whole number.

4. surface area	5. surface area	6. lateral area
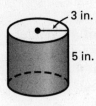 3 in. 5 in.	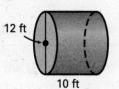 12 ft 10 ft	1 m 2 m

Surface Area of Pyramids and Cones

Goal Find the surface areas of pyramids and cones.

VOCABULARY

Pyramid

Height of a pyramid

Slant height of a pyramid

Cone

Height of a cone

Slant height of a cone

Example 1   *Find the Slant Height*

Find the slant height of the Rainforest
Pyramid. Its base is a square. Round your
answer to the nearest whole number.

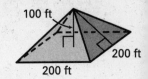

100 ft

200 ft

200 ft

Solution

To find the slant height, use the right triangle formed by the height
and half of the base.

$$(\text{slant height})^2 = (\text{height})^2 + \left(\frac{1}{2}\,\text{side}\right)^2$$ _____

_____

$$= (\underline{})^2 + (\underline{})^2$$ **Substitute values.**

$$= \underline{}$$ **Simplify.**

$$\text{slant height} = \underline{}$$ **Take** _____

_____ .

$$\approx \underline{}$$ **Use a calculator.**

Answer The slant height is about _____ .

SURFACE AREA OF A PYRAMID

Words The surface area of a pyramid is the sum of
the area of a _____ and one-half the product of the
_____ of the base and the _____ .

B

Symbols S =

_____

Example 2   *Find the Surface Area of a Pyramid*

Find the surface area of the pyramid.

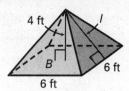

4 ft

l

B

6 ft

6 ft

Solution

1. Find the area of the base.

$$B = s^2 = (\underline{})^2 = \underline{} \ ft^2$$

2. Find the perimeter of the base.

$$P = 4s = 4(\underline{}) = \underline{} \ ft$$

3. Find the slant height of the prism.

$$l^2 = h^2 + \left(\frac{1}{2}s\right)^2 \qquad \underline{}$$

$$= (\underline{})^2 + \left(\frac{1}{2} \cdot \underline{}\right)^2 \qquad \text{Substitute} \ \underline{} \ \text{for } h \text{ and } \underline{} \text{ for } s.$$

$$= \underline{} \qquad\qquad \text{Simplify.}$$

$$l = \underline{} = \underline{} \qquad \text{Take} \ \underline{}.$$

4. Use the formula for the surface area of a pyramid.

$$S = B + \frac{1}{2}Pl \qquad\qquad \text{Formula for surface area}$$

$$= \underline{} + \frac{1}{2}(\underline{})(\underline{}) \qquad \text{Substitute.}$$

$$= \underline{} \qquad\qquad \text{Simplify.}$$

Answer The surface area of the pyramid is $\underline{}$.

✓ *Checkpoint* Find the surface area of the pyramid.

1.	**2.**	**3.**
9 in. 7 in. 7 in.	12 cm 9 cm $B \approx 35.1 \ cm^2$	12 ft 10 ft 10 ft

SURFACE AREA OF A CONE

Words The surface area of a right cone is the sum of the area of the _____ and the product of __, the _____ of the base, and the _____ .

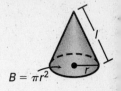

$B = \pi r^2$

Symbols $S = $ _____ or $S = $ _____

Example 3 *Find the Surface Area of a Cone*

Find the surface area of the cone to the nearest whole number.

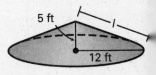

5 ft

12 ft

Solution

Find the slant height.

$(\text{slant height})^2 = r^2 + h^2$ **Pythagorean Theorem**

$= (\underline{})^2 + (\underline{})^2$ **Substitute values.**

$= \underline{}$ **Simplify.**

$\text{slant height} = \underline{} = \underline{}$ **Take the _____ .**

Find the surface area. Use a calculator.

$S = \pi r^2 + \pi r l$ **Formula for surface area**

$= \pi(\underline{})^2 + \pi(\underline{})(\underline{})$ **Substitute values.**

$= \underline{}\pi$ **Simplify.**

$\approx \underline{}$ **Multiply.**

Answer The surface area is about _____ .

✓ **Checkpoint** Find the surface area of the cone to the neares whole number.

4.	5.	6.
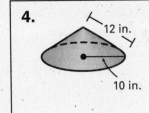 12 in. 10 in.	8 ft 8 ft	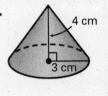 4 cm 3 cm

9.4 Volume of Prisms and Cylinders

Goal Find the volumes of prisms and cylinders.

VOCABULARY

Volume

Example 1 *Find the Volume of a Rectangular Prism*

Find the volume of the box by determining how many unit cubes will fit in the box.

unit cube — 1, 1, 1

Solution

The base is ___ units by ___ units
So, ___ • ___ , or ___ unit cubes are needed to cover the base layer.

There are ___ layers. each layer has ___ cubes. So, the total number of cubes is ___ • ___ , or ___ cubic units.

Answer The volume of the box is ___ cubic units.

4 units
3 units
5 units

Follow-Up Does the amount of each refer to *area* or *volume*?

Paint on a wall	_____
Paint in a can	_____
Wrapping paper on a box	_____
Contents of a box	_____
Water in a lake	_____
Surface covered by a lake	_____

VOLUME OF A PRISM

Words The volume of a prism is the product of the area of the _____ and the _____.

Symbols $V =$ ____

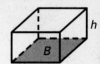

Example 2   *Find the Volume of a Prism*

Find the volume of the prism.

a.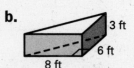

5 in.

4 in.

7 in.

b.

3 ft

6 ft

8 ft

Solution

a. $V = Bh$ Formula for volume of a prism

$= (\_\_ \cdot \_\_) \cdot \_\_$ Area of rectangular base $= l \cdot w = \_\_ \cdot \_\_$

$= \_\_$ Simplify.

Answer The volume of the prism is _____.

b. $V = Bh$ Formula for volume of a prism

$= \left(\dfrac{}{\_\_} \cdot \_\_ \cdot \_\_\right) \cdot \_\_$ Area of a triangular base $=$

$\dfrac{}{\_\_} \cdot \_\_ \cdot \_\_ .$

$= \_\_$ Simplify.

Answer The volume of the prism is _____.

Follow-Up

In Example 2, what is the shape of each base?

a. _____   b. _____

Why do you need to determine the shape of the base to find the volume of a prism?

✓ **Checkpoint** Find the volume of the prism.

1. 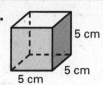 6 ft / 9 ft / 4 ft	**2.** 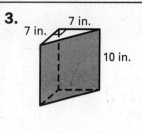 5 cm / 5 cm / 5 cm	**3.** 7 in. / 7 in. / 10 in.

VOLUME OF A CYLINDER

Words The volume of a cylinder is the product
of the area of the _____ and the _____.

Symbols $V =$ ____ = _____

h

B • *r*

Example 3 *Find the Volume of a Cylinder*

Which cylinder has the
greater volume?

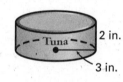

Orange
Juice 6 in.

2 in.

Tuna 2 in.

3 in.

Solution

1. Find the volume of the can of orange juice. Use the formula
   for the volume of a cylinder with $r =$ ___ and $h =$ ___.

   $V = \pi r^2 h = \pi(\_\_)^2(\_\_) = \_\_\_ \pi \approx _____$

2. Find the volume of the can of tuna. Use the formula
   for the volume of a cylinder with $r =$ ___ and $h =$ ___.

   $V = \pi r^2 h = \pi(\_\_)^2(\_\_) = \_\_\_ \pi \approx _____$

3. Compare the volumes of the two cans.

   _____ > _____

Answer The _____ can has the greater volume.

✓ *Checkpoint* **Find the volume of the cylinder. Round your answe**
to the nearest whole number.

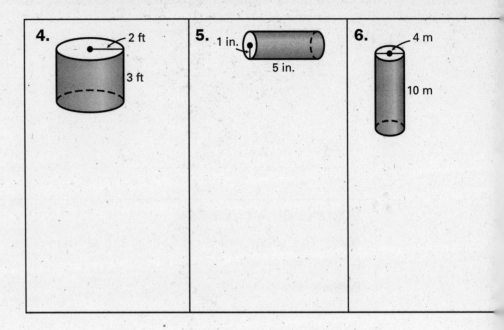

4.

    2 ft

    3 ft

5. 1 in.

    5 in.

6. 4 m

    10 m

9.5 Volume of Pyramids and Cones

Goal Find the volumes of pyramids and cones.

VOLUME OF A PYRAMID

Words The volume of a pyramid is _____ the product of the area of the _____ and the _____ .

Symbols $V =$ _____

Follow-Up

Write the formula for the volume of a prism. _____

Write the formula for the volume of a pyramid.

_____

In both formulas, what does B represent? _____

In both formulas, what does h represent? _____

Which two formulas in this chapter use *slant height* rather than *height*? _____

Example 1   *Find the Volume of a Pyramid*

Find the volume of the pyramid.

a.
6 ft
5 ft
4 ft

b.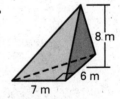
8 m
6 m
7 m

Solution

a. $V = \dfrac{1}{3}Bh$

$= \dfrac{1}{3}(\underline{\quad})(\underline{\quad})$

$= \underline{\quad}$ cubic feet

b. $V = \dfrac{1}{3}Bh$

$= \dfrac{1}{3}\left(\dfrac{\quad}{\quad} \cdot \underline{\quad} \cdot \underline{\quad}\right)(\underline{\quad})$

$= \underline{\quad}$ cubic meters

✔ *Checkpoint* **Find the volume of the pyramid.**

1.	**2.**	**3.**
7 in. 6 in. 6 in.	5 ft 9 ft 8 ft	10 cm 12 cm 9 cm

VOLUME OF A CONE

Words The volume of a cone is _____
the product of the area of the _____ and
the _____ .

Symbols $V =$ _____ = _____

Follow-Up **Complete the statements using** *prism, pyramid, cylinde*
and *cone.*

You can use the formula $V = Bh$ to find the volume of a _____
and _____ .

You can use the formula $V = \frac{1}{3}Bh$ to find the volume of a
_____ and _____ .

The volume of a pyramid is one-third the volume of a _____
with the same height and base.

The volume of a cone is one-third the volume of a _____
with the same height and base.

Example 2   *Find the Volume of a Cone*

Find the volume of the cone. Round your answer to the nearest whole number.

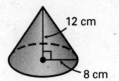

12 cm

8 cm

Solution

The radius of the cone is $r =$ _____.

The height of the cone is $h =$ _____.

$V = \dfrac{1}{3}\pi r^2 h$ **Formula for volume of a cone**

$ = \dfrac{1}{3}\pi(\underline{})^2(\underline{})$ **Substitute** ___ **for** r **and** ___ **for** h.

$ \approx$ _____   **Multiply.**

Answer The volume is about _____.

Example 3   *Find the Volume of a Cone*

What is the volume of the cone shown at the right?

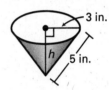

3 in.

h 5 in.

Solution

You are given the _____ and the _____ of the cone.
You need to find the _____ of the cone to find its volume.

1. Find the height of the cone.

$r^2 + h^2 = l^2$ **Use the Pythagorean Theorem.**

$(\underline{})^2 + h^2 = (\underline{})^2$ **Substitute given lengths.**

$\underline{} + h^2 = \underline{}$ **Simplify.**

$h^2 = \underline{}$ **Subtract** ___ **from each side.**

$h = \underline{}$ **Take the positive square root.**

2. Find the volume of the cone.

$V = \dfrac{1}{3}\pi r^2 h = \dfrac{1}{3}\pi(\underline{})^2(\underline{}) \approx \underline{}$

Answer The volume of the cone is about _____.

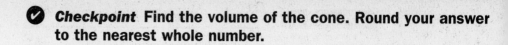

✓ Checkpoint Find the volume of the cone. Round your answer to the nearest whole number.

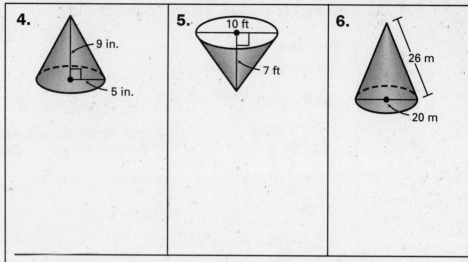

4. 9 in. 5 in.

5. 10 ft 7 ft

6. 26 m 20 m

7. Find the volume of a cone with a height of 6 inches and a diameter of 8 inches.

8. Find the volume of a cone with a slant height of 17 feet and a diameter of 16 feet.

9.6 Surface Area and Volume of Spheres

Goal Find the surface areas and volumes of spheres.

VOCABULARY

Sphere

Hemisphere

Follow-Up **Circle the words that differ in the definitions below.**

A circle is the set of all points in a plane that are the same distance from a given point, called the center.

A sphere is the set of all points in space that are the same distance from a given point, called the center.

Draw the figures described below.

A circle with center C and radius 6 centimeters.	A sphere with center S and radius 6 centimeters.

SURFACE AREA OF A SPHERE

Words The surface area of a sphere is
_____ times pi times the square of the
_____ .

Symbols $S =$ _____

center   radius

Example 1 *Find the Surface Area of a Sphere*

Find the surface area of the sphere. Round your answer to the nearest whole number.

a.

b.

Solution

a. The radius is 8 inches, so $r =$ ___ .

$$S = 4\pi r^2 = 4 \cdot \pi \cdot (\underline{})^2 \approx \underline{}$$

b. The diameter is 10 centimeters, so the radius is $r =$ ___ .

$$S = 4\pi r^2 = 4 \cdot \pi \cdot (\underline{})^2 \approx \underline{}$$

✔ **Checkpoint** Find the surface area of the sphere. Round your answer to the nearest whole number.

1.	2.	3.

VOLUME OF A SPHERE

Words The volume of a sphere is _____ the product of pi and the cube of the _____ .

Symbols $V =$ _____

Follow-Up Complete the following statements.

> For the surface area of a sphere, the radius is _____ and the units are _____.
>
> For the volume of a sphere, the radius is _____ and the units are _____.

Example 2   *Find the Volume of a Sphere*

Find the volume of the sphere or hemisphere. Round your answer to the nearest whole number.

a. 2 ft

b. 5 in.

Solution

a. $V = \dfrac{4}{3}\pi r^3$ Formula for volume of a sphere

$ = \dfrac{4}{3} \cdot \pi \cdot (\underline{})^3$ Substitute ___ for *r*.

$ \approx \underline{}$ Simplify.

b. A hemisphere has _____ the volume of a sphere.

$V = \underline{} \cdot \dfrac{4}{3}\pi r^3$ Formula for _____ the volume of a sphere

$ = \underline{} \cdot \dfrac{4}{3} \cdot \pi \cdot (\underline{})^3$ Substitute ___ for *r*.

$ \approx \underline{}$ Simplify.

Example 3 *Find the Volume of a Sphere*

Estimate the volume of air in a beach ball that
has a 12-inch diameter. Round to the nearest
whole number.

Solution

$$V = \frac{4}{3}\pi r^3 \qquad \text{Write volume formula.}$$

$$= \frac{4}{3} \cdot \pi \cdot (\underline{\hspace{0.5cm}})^3 \qquad \text{Substitute \underline{\hspace{0.3cm}} for } r.$$

$$\approx \underline{\hspace{1.5cm}} \qquad \text{Simplify.}$$

Answer The volume of air in the ball is about _____.

✓ *Checkpoint* **Find the volume of the solid to the nearest whole number.**

4.	5.	6.
4 in.	3 cm	18 ft

Follow-Up For each solid you have learned in this chapter, write the two formulas. Then draw and label a diagram.

Solid	Surface Area	Volume	Diagram
Prism			
Cylinder			
Pyramid			
Cone			
Sphere			

Words to Review

Give an example of the vocabulary word.

Solid	Polyhedron, face, edge
Prism, base, lateral faces	Surface area
Cylinder	Pyramid, height, slant height
Cone, height, slant height	Volume of a solid

Sphere	Hemisphere

Review your notes and Chapter 9 by using the Chapter Summary and Review on pages 524–527 of your textbook.

Simplifying Square Roots

Goal Simplify square roots.

VOCABULARY

Radical

Radicand

Example 1 *Use a Calculator to Find Square Roots*

Find the square root of 52. Round your answer to the nearest tenth. Check that your answer is reasonable.

Using a calculator, $\sqrt{52}$ is _____. This number rounded to the nearest tenth is ____.

Because 52 is between the two perfect squares ____ and ____, $\sqrt{52}$ should be between _____ and _____, or ___ and ___. The answer is between ___ and ___, so it is reasonable.

Example 2 *Find Side Lengths*

Use the Pythagorean Theorem to find the length of the hypotenuse to the nearest tenth.

$$a^2 + b^2 = c^2 \qquad \text{Pythagorean Theorem}$$

$$(\underline{\quad})^2 + (\underline{\quad})^2 = c^2 \qquad \text{Substitute.}$$

$$\underline{\quad} + \underline{\quad} = c^2 \qquad \text{Simplify.}$$

$$\underline{\quad} = c^2 \qquad \text{Add.}$$

$$\underline{\quad\quad} = c \qquad \text{Take the square root of each side.}$$

$$\underline{\quad\quad} \approx c \qquad \text{Use a calculator.}$$

(right triangle with legs labeled $\sqrt{2}$ and $\sqrt{3}$, hypotenuse labeled c)

Example 3 Multiply Radicals

Multiply the radicals. Then simplify if possible.

a. $\sqrt{3} \cdot \sqrt{7}$ b. $\sqrt{2} \cdot \sqrt{8}$

Solution

Use the Product Property of Radicals.

a. $\sqrt{3} \cdot \sqrt{7} = \sqrt{\underline{\hspace{1cm}}}$ b. $\sqrt{2} \cdot \sqrt{8} = \sqrt{\underline{\hspace{1cm}}}$

          $= \underline{\hspace{1cm}}$ $= \underline{\hspace{1cm}}$

                                                     $= \underline{\hspace{1cm}}$

Follow-Up

In Example 3, why is it possible to simplify $\sqrt{16}$ but not possible to simplify $\sqrt{21}$?

Example 4 Simplify Radicals

Simplify the radical expression.

a. $\sqrt{12}$ b. $\sqrt{45}$

Solution

a. $\sqrt{12} = \sqrt{\underline{\hspace{1cm}}}$ b. $\sqrt{45} = \sqrt{\underline{\hspace{1cm}}}$

        $= \underline{\hspace{1.5cm}}$ $= \underline{\hspace{1.5cm}}$

        $= \underline{\hspace{1cm}}$ $= \underline{\hspace{1cm}}$

✔ Checkpoint **Find the square root. Round your answer to the nearest tenth. Check that your answer is reasonable.**

1. $\sqrt{27}$	2. $\sqrt{46}$	3. $\sqrt{8}$	4. $\sqrt{97}$

Multiply the radicals. Then simplify if possible.

5. $\sqrt{3} \cdot \sqrt{5}$	6. $\sqrt{11} \cdot \sqrt{6}$
7. $\sqrt{3} \cdot \sqrt{27}$	8. $5\sqrt{3} \cdot \sqrt{3}$

Simplify the radical expression.

9. $\sqrt{20}$	10. $\sqrt{8}$
11. $\sqrt{75}$	12. $\sqrt{112}$

10.2 45°-45°-90° Triangles

Goal Find the side lengths of 45°-45°-90° triangles.

VOCABULARY

45°-45°-90° triangle

THEOREM 10.1: 45°-45°-90° TRIANGLE THEOREM

Words In a 45°-45°-90° triangle, the length of the
hypotenuse is the length of a leg times ____.

Symbols hypotenuse = leg · ____

Example 1 *Find Hypotenuse Length*

Find the length x of the hypotenuse in the
45°-45°-90° triangle shown at the right.

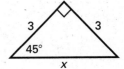

Solution

By the 45°-45°-90° Triangle Theorem, the length of the hypotenuse
is the length of a leg times ____.

   hypotenuse = leg · ____   **45°-45°-90° Triangle Theorem**

            = _____   **Substitute.**

Answer The length of the hypotenuse is _____.

Example 2   Find Leg Length

Find the length x of each leg in the 45°-45°-90° triangle shown at the right.

Solution

hypotenuse = leg · $\sqrt{2}$	45°-45°-90° Triangle Theorem
_____ = _____	Substitute.
$\dfrac{\quad}{\quad} = \dfrac{\quad}{\quad}$	Divide each side by ____.
__ = x	Simplify.

Answer The length of each leg is __.

✔ **Checkpoint** Find the value of x.

1.

2.

Example 3   Identify 45°-45°-90° Triangles

Determine whether there is enough information to conclude that the triangle is a 45°-45°-90° triangle. Explain your reasoning.

Solution

By the Triangle Sum Theorem, $x° + x° + 90° = $ _____.

So, $2x° = $ ____, and $x = $ ___.

Answer Since the measure of each acute angle is _____, the triang _____ a 45°-45°-90° triangle.

Follow-Up

Example 3 shows that whenever the acute angles of a right triangle are _____ , the triangle is a _____ triangle.

Example 4 **Find Leg Length**

Show that the triangle is a 45°-45°-90° triangle. Then find the value of x.

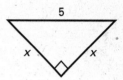

Solution

The triangle is an isosceles right triangle. By the Base Angles Theorem, its acute angles are congruent. From the result of Example 3, this triangle must be a 45°-45°-90° triangle.

hypotenuse = _____   **45°-45°-90° Triangle Theorem**

___ = _____   **Substitute.**

= _____   **Divide each side by ____ .**

$\dfrac{\quad}{\quad}$ $\dfrac{\quad}{\quad}$

_____ = x   **Simplify.**

_____ ≈ x   **Use a calculator to approximate.**

✔ **Checkpoint** Show that the triangle is a 45°-45°-90° triangle. Then find the value of x. Round your answer to the nearest tenth.

3.

8

10.3 30°-60°-90° Triangles

Goal Find the side lengths of 30°-60°-90° triangles.

VOCABULARY

30°-60°-90° triangle

Example 1 *Find Leg Length*

In the diagram, $\triangle PQR$ is a 30°-60°-90° triangle. Find the value of b.

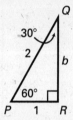

Solution

$(\text{leg})^2 + (\text{leg})^2 =$ _____   Pythagorean Theorem

_____ = ____   Substitute.

_____ = __   Simplify.

___ = __   Subtract ___ from each side.

$b =$ ___   Solve for b.

THEOREM 10.2: 30°-60°-90° TRIANGLE THEOREM

Words In a 30°-60°-90° triangle, the hypotenuse is _____ as long as the shorter leg, and the longer leg is the length of the shorter leg times ____.

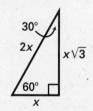

Symbols Hypotenuse = __ • shorter leg

Longer leg = shorter leg • ____

Example 2   *Find Hypotenuse Length*

In the 30°-60°-90° triangle at the right,
the length of the shorter leg is given.
Find the length of the hypotenuse.

Solution

The hypotenuse of a 30°-60°-90° triangle is _____ as long as
the shorter leg.

   hypotenuse = __ • shorter leg   **30°-60°-90° Triangle Theorem**

          = __ • ___   **Substitute.**

          = ____   **Simplify.**

Answer The length of the hypotenuse is ___.

Example 3   *Find Longer Leg Length*

In the 30°-60°-90° triangle at the right,
the length of the shorter leg is given.
Find the length of the longer leg.

Solution

The length of the longer leg of a 30°-60°-90° triangle is the
length of the shorter leg times ____.

   longer leg = shorter leg • ____   **30°-60°-90° Triangle Theorem**

          = __ • ____   **Substitute.**

Answer The length of the longer leg is _____.

Follow-Up

In a 30°-60°-90° triangle, the longer leg is opposite the ____
angle, and the shorter leg is opposite the ____ angle.

✔ **Checkpoint** Find the value of *x*. Write your answer in radical form.

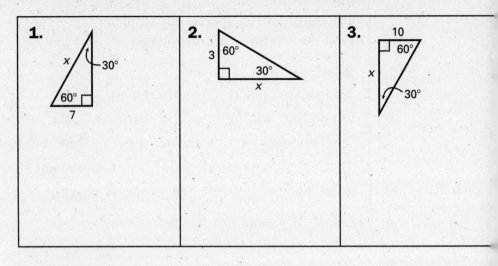

1.	2.	3.

Example 4   *Find Shorter Leg Length*

In the 30°-60°-90° triangle at the right, the length of the longer leg is given. Find the length *x* of the shorter leg. Round your answer to the nearest tenth.

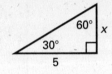

Solution

The length of a longer leg of a 30°-60°-90° triangle is the length of a shorter leg times _____.

longer leg = _____ • ____   30°-60°-90° Triangle Theorem

___ = _____   Substitute.

= ___   Divide each side by _____.
_____

_____ ≈ *x*   Use a calculator to approximate.

Answer The length of the shorter leg is about _____.

Follow-Up

In Example 4, what is the length of the hypotenuse?

Example 5 *Find Leg Lengths*

In the 30°-60°-90° triangle at the right, the length of the hypotenuse is given. Find the length *x* of the shorter leg and the length *y* of the longer leg.

Solution

Use the 30°-60°-90° Triangle Theorem to find the length of the shorter leg. Then use that value to find the length of the longer leg.

Shorter leg	Longer leg

hypotenuse = __ • _____   longer leg = _____ • __

__ = _____   *y* = _____

__ = *x*   *y* = _____

Answer The length of the shorter leg is __. The length of the longer leg is _____.

✓ *Checkpoint* **Find the value of each variable. Round your answer to the nearest tenth.**

4.

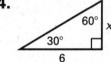

5.

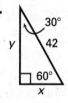

10.4 Tangent Ratio

Goal Find the tangent of an acute angle.

VOCABULARY

Trigonometric ratio

_____

Tangent

TANGENT RATIO

For any acute angle A of a right triangle:

$$\tan A = \frac{\text{leg opposite } \angle A}{\text{leg adjacent to } \angle A} = \underline{\quad\quad}$$

The tangent of angle A is written as "tan A."

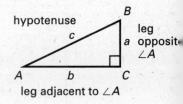

hypotenuse c

leg a opposite $\angle A$

leg adjacent to $\angle A$

Example 1 *Find Tangent Ratio*

Find tan S and tan R as fractions in simplified form and as decimals rounded to four decimal places.

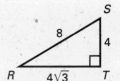

Solution

$$\tan S = \frac{\text{leg opposite } \angle S}{\text{leg adjacent } \angle S} = \underline{\quad} = \underline{\quad} \approx \underline{\quad}$$

$$\tan R = \frac{\text{leg opposite } \angle R}{\text{leg adjacent to } \angle R} = \underline{\quad} = \underline{\quad} \approx \underline{\quad}$$

Follow-Up

In Example 1, what is the relationship between tan *S* and tan *R*?

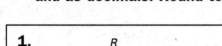

Approximate tan 74° to four decimal places.

Solution

Using the TAN function on the calculator, tan 74° is _____.
This number rounded to four decimal places is _____.

✓ *Checkpoint* Find tan *S* and tan *R* as fractions in simplified form
and as decimals. Round to four decimal places if necessary.

1. 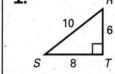	2. 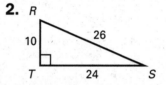

Use a calculator to approximate the value to four decimal places.

3. tan 35°	4. tan 85°	5. tan 10°

Example 3   *Find Leg Length*

Use a tangent ratio to find the value of x.
Round your answer to the nearest tenth.

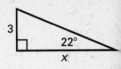

3

22°

x

Solution

$\tan 22° = $ _____   **Write the tangent ratio.**

$\tan 22° = \dfrac{}{}$ **Substitute.**

_____ $= $ ___   **Multiply each side by __.**

___ $= \dfrac{}{}$ **Divide each side by tan ____.**

$x \approx \dfrac{}{}$ **Use an approximate value for**
                                      _____.

$x \approx$ _____   **Simplify.**

Example 4   *Find Leg Length*

Use two different tangent ratios to find the value
of x to the nearest tenth.

35°

x

Solution

First, find the measure of the other acute angle:
$90° - $ _____ $= $ _____.

Method 1	Method 2

$\tan 35° = $ _____ $\tan 55° = $ _____

$\tan 35° = \dfrac{}{}$ $\tan 55° = \dfrac{}{}$

_____ $= \dfrac{}{}$ _____ $= x$

$x = \dfrac{}{}$ _____ $\approx x$

$x \approx$ _____

Example 5 *Estimate Height*

You stand 45 feet from the base of a tree and look up at the top of the tree as shown in the diagram. Use a tangent ratio to estimate the height of the tree to the nearest foot.

Solution

$$\tan 59° = \underline{\hspace{3cm}}$$ Write ratio.

$$\tan 59° = \underline{\hspace{1.5cm}}$$ Substitute.

$$\underline{\hspace{2cm}} = \underline{\hspace{1cm}}$$ Multiply each side by ____.

$$\underline{\hspace{1.5cm}} \approx h$$ Use a calculator.

Answer The tree is about _____ tall.

✓ *Checkpoint* Write two equations you can use to find the value of *x*.

6.	7.	8.

9. Find the value of *x*. Round your answer to the nearest tenth.

10.5 Sine and Cosine Ratios

Goal Find the sine and cosine of an acute angle.

VOCABULARY

Sine

Cosine

SINE AND COSINE RATIOS

For any acute angle A of a
right triangle:

$$\sin A = \frac{\text{leg opposite } \angle A}{\text{hypotenuse}} = \underline{\quad}$$

$$\cos A = \frac{\text{leg adjacent to } \angle A}{\text{hypotenuse}} = \underline{\quad}$$

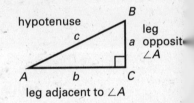

Example 1 *Find Sine and Cosine Ratios*

Find sin A and cos A.

Solution

sin A = ─────────────   **Write ratio for sine.**

= ──   **Substitute.**

cos A = ─────────────   **Write ratio for cosine.**

= ──   **Substitute.**

✓ Checkpoint Find sin *A* and cos *A*.

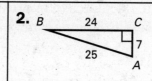

1.	2.	3.

Example 2 **Find Sine and Cosine Ratios**

Find sin *A* and cos *A*. Write your answers
as fractions and as decimals rounded to
four decimal places.

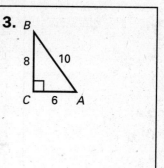

Solution

sin *A* = _____ = ____ ≈ _____

cos *A* = _____ = ____ ≈ _____

✓ Checkpoint Find sin *A* and cos *A*. Write your answers as
fractions and as decimals rounded to four decimal places.

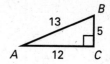

4.	5.	6.

Example 3   Use a Calculator for Sine and Cosine

Use a calculator to approximate sin 74° and cos 74°. Round your answers to four decimal places.

Solution

Using the SIN function on your calculator, sin 74° is _____

This number rounded to four decimal places is _____.

Using the COS function on your calculator, cos 74° is _____

This number rounded to four decimal places is _____.

✔ **Checkpoint** Use a calculator to approximate the value to four decimal places.

7. sin 43°	8. cos 43°	9. sin 15°	10. cos 15°

Example 4   Find Leg Lengths

Find the lengths of the legs of the triangle. Round your answers to the nearest tenth.

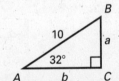

Solution

$$\sin 32° = \frac{}{}$$ $$\cos 32° = \frac{}{}$$

$$\frac{\qquad}{} = \frac{}{}$$ $$\frac{\qquad}{} = \frac{}{}$$

$$\frac{\qquad}{} \approx \frac{}{}$$ $$\frac{\qquad}{} \approx \frac{}{}$$

$$\underline{\qquad} \approx a$$ $$\underline{\qquad} \approx b$$

Answer In the triangle, BC is about _____ and AC is about _____.

✔ **Checkpoint** Find the lengths of the legs of the triangle. Round your answers to the nearest tenth.

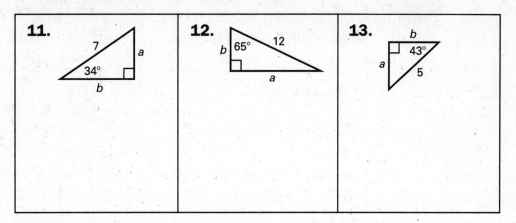

11.

7   a

34°

b

12.

b 65°   12

a

13.

b

43°

a

5

Follow-Up Complete the table for any acute angle *A* of a right triangle.

tan A = _____ = ___

        B
      c   a
   A   b   C

sin A = $\dfrac{\boxed{}}{\text{hypotenuse}}$ = ___

        B
      c   a
   A   b   C

cos A = $\dfrac{\boxed{}}{\text{hypotenuse}}$ = ___

        B
      c   a
   A   b   C

10.6 Solving Right Triangles

Goal Solve a right triangle.

VOCABULARY

Solve a right triangle

Inverse tangent

Inverse sine

Inverse cosine

INVERSE TANGENT

For any acute angle A of a right triangle:

    If $\tan A = z$, then $\tan^{-1} z = $ _____ .

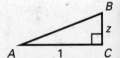

INVERSE SINE AND INVERSE COSINE

For any acute angle A of a right triangle:

    If $\sin A = y$, then $\sin^{-1} y = $ _____ .

    If $\cos A = x$, then $\cos^{-1} x = $ _____ .

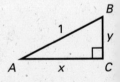

Example 1   *Use Inverse Tangent*

Use a calculator to approximate the measure of $\angle A$ to the nearest tenth of a degree.

Solution

Because $\tan A =$ _____ $=$ _____ , $\tan^{-1}$ _____ $= m\angle A$.

Using the inverse tangent function on the calculator, the inverse tangent of 0.8 is _____. This number rounded to the nearest tenth is _____. So, $m\angle A \approx$ _____.

Follow-Up

Explain how to use the table of trigonometric ratios in your textbook to find $m\angle A$ in Example 1.

Example 2   *Solve a Right Triangle*

Find each measure to the nearest tenth.

a. c **b.** $m\angle B$

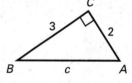

Solution

a. $(\text{hypotenuse})^2 = (\text{leg})^2 + (\text{leg})^2$ **Pythagorean Theorem**

_____ $=$ _____ $+$ _____   **Substitute.**

_____ $=$ _____   **Simplify.**

_____ $=$ _____   **Find the positive square root.**

$c \approx$ _____   **Use a calculator.**

b. Use a calculator to find $m\angle B$.

Because $\tan B =$ _____ $\approx$ _____ , $m\angle B \approx \tan^{-1}$ _____ $\approx$ _____

Checkpoint ∠A is an acute angle. Use a calculator to approximate the measure of ∠A to the nearest tenth of a degree.

1. tan A = 3.5	**2.** tan A = 2	**3.** tan A = 0.4402

Find the measure of ∠A.

4. 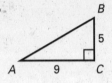	**5.**	**6.** 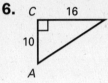

Example 3   *Find the Measures of Acute Angles*

∠A is an acute angle. Use a calculator to approximate the meas
of ∠A to the nearest tenth of a degree.

a. sin A = 0.55   **b.** cos A = 0.48

Solution

a. Because sin A = 0.55, m∠A = sin⁻¹ _____.

   sin⁻¹ _____ ≈ _____, so m∠A ≈ _____.

b. Because cos A = 0.48, m∠A = cos⁻¹ _____.

   cos⁻¹ _____ ≈ _____, so m∠A ≈ _____.

Example 4 **Solve a Right Triangle**

Solve △*GHJ* by finding each measure.
Round decimals to the nearest tenth.

a. *m∠G*   **b.** *m∠H*   **c.** *g*

Solution

a. Because cos *G* = _____ = _____ , *m∠G* = _____ .

_____ ≈ _____ so, *m∠G* ≈ _____

b. ∠*G* and ∠*H* are complementary.

m∠H = 90° − _____ = _____ = _____ .

c. _____ = (hypotenuse)²   **Pythagorean Theorem**

_____ = _____   **Substitute.**

_____ = _____   **Simplify.**

_____ = _____   **Subtract _____ from each side.**

_____ = _____   **Find the positive square root.**

g ≈ _____   **Use a calculator.**

✔ *Checkpoint* ∠*A* is an acute angle. Use a calculator to approximate the measure of ∠*A* to the nearest tenth of a degree.

7. sin *A* = 0.5	**8.** cos *A* = 0.92	**9.** sin *A* = 0.1149

Solve the right triangle. Round decimals to the nearest tenth.

10.	**11.**	**12.**

Words to Review

Give an example of the vocabulary word.

Radical, radicand	45°-45°-90° triangle
30°-60°-90° triangle	Trigonometric ratio
Tangent	Sine
Cosine	Solve a right triangle

Inverse tangent	Inverse sine

Inverse cosine

Review your notes and Chapter 10 by using the Chapter Summary and Review on pages 576–579 of your textbook.

11.1 Parts of a Circle

Goal Identify segments and lines related to circles.

VOCABULARY

Chord

Secant

Tangent, point of tangency

Follow-Up Categorize each of the following terms: *center, radius, diameter, chord, secant, tangent, point of tangency.*

Points	Segments	Lines

Example 1 *Identify Special Segments and Lines*

Tell whether the line or segment is best described as a *chord*, a *secant*, a *tangent*, a *diameter*, or a *radius* of $\odot C$.

a. $\overline{AD}$ b. $\overline{HB}$ c. $\overleftrightarrow{EG}$

Solution

a. $\overline{AD}$ is a _____ because _____

_____ .

b. $\overline{HB}$ is a _____ because _____ .

c. $\overleftrightarrow{EG}$ is a _____ because _____

_____ .

Follow-Up Use the diagram in Example 1 to name the following parts.

The center of the circle ___

A point of tangency ___

Two radii (plural for radius) _____

Three chords _____

Draw each diagram described below.

⊙A with diameters $\overline{BC}$ and $\overline{DE}$	⊙F with tangent $\overleftrightarrow{GH}$ and secant $\overleftrightarrow{HJ}$

Example 2   *Name Special Segments, Lines, and Points*

Identify a chord, a secant, a tangent, a diameter, two radii, the center, and a point of tangency.

Solution

_____ is a chord.   _____ is a secant.

_____ is a tangent.   _____ is a diameter.

_____ is a radius.   _____ is a radius.

___ is the center.   ___ is a point of tangency.

Follow-Up

In Example 2, is $\overline{DE}$ a *chord* or a *diameter*? Explain.

Example 3   *Circles in Coordinate Geometry*

When a circle lies in a coordinate plane, you can use coordinates to describe particular points of the circle.

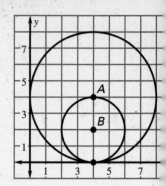

a. Name the coordinates of the center of each circle.

b. Name the coordinates of the intersection of the two circles.

c. What is the line that is tangent to both circles? Name the coordinates of the point of tangency.

d. What is the length of the diameter of ⊙B? What is the length of the radius of ⊙A?

Solution

a. The center of ⊙A is A(__, __). The center of ⊙B is B(__, __).

b. The intersection of the two circles is the point (__, __).

c. The __-axis is tangent to both circles. The point of tangency is (__, __).

d. The length of the diameter of ⊙B is __. The length of the radiu of ⊙A is __.

✔ *Checkpoint* Complete the following exercises.

1. Identify a chord, a secant, a tangent, a diameter, a radius, the center, and a point of tangency.

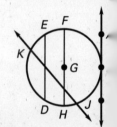

2. In Example 3, name the point of tangency of the y-axis to ⊙A.

11.2 Properties of Tangents

Goal Use properties of a tangent to a circle.

VOCABULARY

Tangent segment

THEOREM 11.1

Words If a line is tangent to a circle, then it is
_____ to the radius drawn at the
_____.

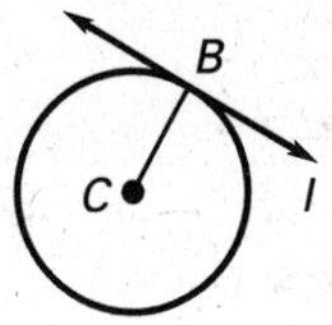

Symbols If *l* is tangent to ⊙*C* at *B*, then _____.

THEOREM 11.2

Words In a plane, if a line is _____ to
a radius of a circle at its endpoint on the circle,
then the line is _____ to the circle.

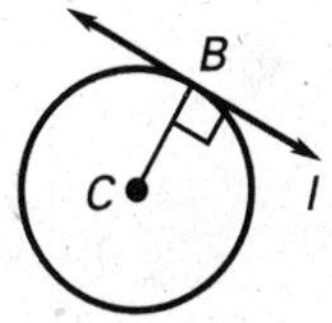

Symbols If _____, then *l* is tangent to ⊙*C* at *B*.

Follow-Up

What is the relationship between Theorems 11.1 and 11.2?

The word *tangent* is based on a Latin word meaning "to touch."
How does this relate to the definition of tangent?

Example 1   Use Properties of Tangents

$\overrightarrow{AC}$ is tangent to $\odot B$ at point C. Find BC.

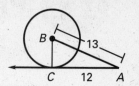

Solution

$\overline{BC}$ is a _____ of $\odot B$, so you can apply Theorem 11.1 to conclude
that $\overline{BC}$ and $\overrightarrow{AC}$ are _____.

So, $\angle BCA$ is a _____ angle, and $\triangle BCA$ is a _____ triangle. To find
BC, use _____.

$$(BA)^2 = (BC)^2 + (CA)^2$$

$(\_\_)^2 = (BC)^2 + (\_\_)^2$ **Substitute given lengths.**

$\_\_ = (BC)^2 + \_\_$ **Multiply.**

$\_\_ = (BC)^2$ **Subtract** _____ **from each side.**

$\_\_ = BC$ **Find the positive** _____.

Example 2   Find the Radius of a Circle

You are standing at C, 8 feet from
a grain silo. The distance to a point
of tangency is 16 feet. What is the
radius of the silo?

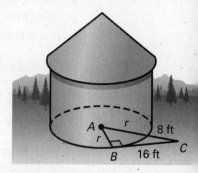

Solution

Tangent $\overleftrightarrow{BC}$ is _____ to radius $\overline{AB}$ at B, so $\triangle ABC$ is a
_____ triangle. So, you can use _____.

$$(AC)^2 = (AB)^2 + (BC)^2$$

$(\_\_ + \_\_)^2 = (\_\_)^2 + (\_\_)^2$ **Substitute given lengths.**

$_____ = \_\_ + \_\_$ **Multiply.**

$\_\_\_\_\_ = \_\_\_\_\_$ **Subtract** ___ **from each side.**

$\_\_\_\_\_ = \_\_\_\_\_$ **Subtract** ___ **from each side.**

$r = \_\_\_$ **Divide each side by** ___.

Answer The radius of the silo is _____.

Example 3 *Verify a Tangent to a Circle*

How can you show that $\overleftrightarrow{EF}$ must
be tangent to $\odot D$?

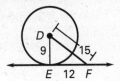

Solution

Use the Converse of the Pythagorean Theorem to determine
whether $\triangle DEF$ is a _____ triangle.

$(DF)^2 \overset{?}{=} (DE)^2 + (EF)^2$ Compare $(DF)^2$ with $(DE)^2 + (EF)^2$.

$\underline{\quad}^2 \overset{?}{=} \underline{\quad}^2 + \underline{\quad}^2$ Substitute given lengths.

$\underline{\quad} \overset{?}{=} \underline{\quad} + \underline{\quad}$ Multiply.

$\underline{\quad} \ \underline{\quad} \ \underline{\quad}$ Simplify.

$\triangle DEF$ is a _____ triangle with right angle E. So, $\overline{EF}$ is
_____ to $\overline{DE}$. By Theorem _____, it follows that $\overleftrightarrow{EF}$ is
_____ to $\odot D$.

THEOREM 11.3

Words If two segments from the same point
outside a circle are _____ to the circle,
then they are _____.

Symbols If $\overline{SR}$ and $\overline{ST}$ are tangent to $\odot P$ at
points R and T, then _____.

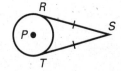

Example 4 *Use Properties of Tangents*

$\overline{AB}$ is tangent to $\odot C$ at B.
$\overline{AD}$ is tangent to $\odot C$ at D.
Find the value of x.

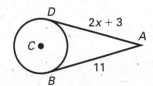

Solution

$\underline{\quad} = \underline{\quad}$ Two tangent segments from the same point are
congruent.

$\underline{\quad} = \underline{\quad}$ Substitute _____ for AD and ___ for AB.

$\underline{\quad} = \underline{\quad}$ Subtract ___ from each side.

$\underline{\quad} = \underline{\quad}$ Divide each side by ___.

Follow-Up

Check your answer for Example 4.

$AD = 2x + 3 = 2(\_\_) + 3 = \_\_ + 3 = \_\_$

Why should *AD* equal 11?

✓ *Checkpoint* $\overline{CB}$ and $\overline{CD}$ are tangent to ⊙A. **Find the value of ⟩**

1.

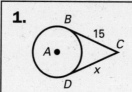

2.

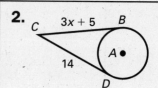

11.3 Arcs and Central Angles

Goal Use properties of arcs of circles.

VOCABULARY

Minor arc, major arc

Measure of a minor arc

Measure of a major arc

Semicircle

Congruent circles

Congruent arcs

Arc length

Follow-Up

Name the type of arc that has the measure described below. Then tell how many points are used to name this type of arc.

Less than 180°   Equal to 180°   Greater than 180°

Example 1   Name and Find Measures of Arcs

Name the gray arc and identify the type of arc. Then find its measure.

a.

b.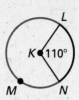

Solution

a. $\overset{\frown}{DF}$ is a _____ arc. Its measure is ____°.

b. $\overset{\frown}{LMN}$ is a _____ arc. Its measure is $360° -$ ____° = ____°.

POSTULATE 16: ARC ADDITION POSTULATE

Words The measure of an arc formed by two adjacent arcs is the _____ of the measures of the two arcs.

Symbols $m\overset{\frown}{ACB} =$ _____

Example 2   Find Measures of Arcs

Find the measure of $\overset{\frown}{GEF}$.

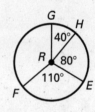

Solution

Use the Arc Addition Postulate.

$m\overset{\frown}{GEF} = m\overset{\frown}{GH} + m\overset{\frown}{HE} + m\overset{\frown}{EF}$

$= $ ___° + ___° + ___°

$= $ ____°

Example 3   *Identifying Congruent Arcs*

Find the measures of the gray arcs. Are the arcs congruent?

a.

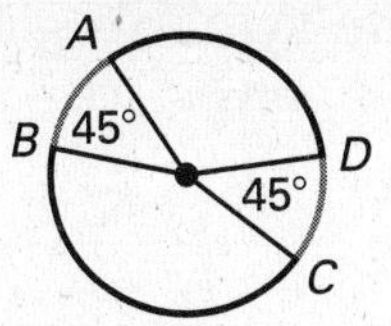

b.
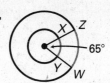

Solution

a. Notice that $\overset{\frown}{AB}$ and $\overset{\frown}{DC}$ are in the same circle. Because $m\overset{\frown}{AB} = m\overset{\frown}{DC} = 45°$, _____ .

b. Notice that $\overset{\frown}{XY}$ and $\overset{\frown}{ZW}$ are not in the same circle or in congruent circles. Therefore, although $m\overset{\frown}{XY} = m\overset{\frown}{ZW} = 65°$,

_____ .

✔ **Checkpoint** Find the measures of the arcs in ⊙A. Are the arcs congruent?

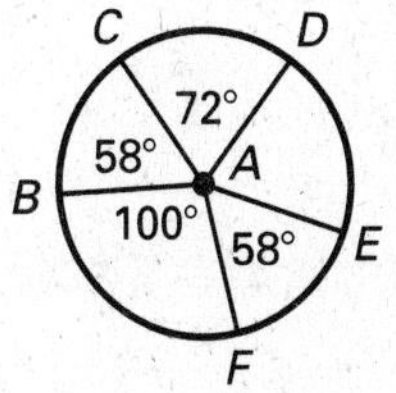

1. $\overset{\frown}{BC}$ and $\overset{\frown}{EF}$ $m\overset{\frown}{BC} =$ ____ $m\overset{\frown}{EF} =$ ____ Congruent? ____	**2.** $\overset{\frown}{BC}$ and $\overset{\frown}{CD}$ $m\overset{\frown}{BC} =$ ____ $m\overset{\frown}{CD} =$ ____ Congruent? ____
3. $\overset{\frown}{CD}$ and $\overset{\frown}{DE}$ $m\overset{\frown}{CD} =$ ____ $m\overset{\frown}{DE} =$ ____ Congruent? ____	**4.** $\overset{\frown}{BFE}$ and $\overset{\frown}{CBF}$ $m\overset{\frown}{BFE} =$ ____ $m\overset{\frown}{CBF} =$ ____ Congruent? ____

(Circle diagram for questions 2–4: points C, D at top; B at left; A center; E at right with 58°; F at bottom. Angles shown: 72°, 58°, 100°, 58°.)

ARC LENGTH COROLLARY

Words In a circle, the ratio of the length of a given arc to the circumference is equal to the ratio of the measure of the arc to _____ .

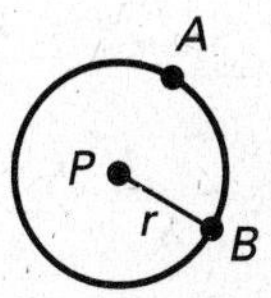

Symbols Arc length of $\overset{\frown}{AB} =$

_____

Follow-Up

Use the words of the Arc Length Corollary to write a proportion. Show that it is equivalent to the symbols given.

Example 4   Find Arc Lengths

Find the length of the gray arc. Round your answer to the nearest hundredth.

a.

b.

c.

Solution

a. Arc length of $\overset{\frown}{AB}$ = _____ $\cdot \; 2\pi(\underline{\ \ }) \approx$ _____

b. Arc length of $\overset{\frown}{CD}$ = _____ $\cdot \; 2\pi(\underline{\ \ }) \approx$ _____

c. Arc length of $\overset{\frown}{EF}$ = _____ $\cdot \; 2\pi(\underline{\ \ }) \approx$ _____

✓ **Checkpoint** Find the length of the gray arc. Round your answ to the nearest hundredth.

5.	6.	7.
	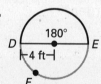	

11.4 Arcs and Chords

Goal Use properties of chords of circles.

THEOREM 11.4

Words If a diameter of a circle is _____ to a chord, then the diameter _____ the chord and its arc.

Symbols If _____, then $\overline{DE} \cong \overline{EF}$ and $\overset{\frown}{DG} \cong \overset{\frown}{GF}$.

Follow-Up Use the diagram for Theorem 11.4.

Name the diameter. _____

Name the chord that the diameter bisects. _____

Name the arc that the diameter bisects. _____

At the right, draw the diagram for Theorem 11.4. Mark all congruent segments and congruent arcs.

Example 1   *Find the Length of a Chord*

In $\odot C$, the diameter $\overline{AF}$ is perpendicular to $\overline{BD}$. Use the diagram to find the length of $\overline{BD}$.

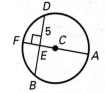

Solution

Because $\overline{AF}$ is a diameter that is perpendicular to $\overline{BD}$, you can use Theorem 11.4 to conclude that _____. So, $BE =$ ____ = __

$BD = BE + ED$ Segment Addition Postulate

    $=$ __ + __   Substitute __ for BE and ED.

    $=$ ____   Simplify.

Answer The length of $\overline{BD}$ is ____.

Name the parts that the diameter bisects in Example 1.

Chord: _____   Arc: _____

Complete two congruence statements for Example 1.

Chords: _____   Arcs: _____

✓ *Checkpoint* **Find the length of the segment.**

1. Find the length of $\overline{JM}$.

2. Find the length of $\overline{SR}$.

THEOREM 11.5

Words If one chord is a perpendicular bisector of another chord, then the first chord is a _____.

Symbols If $\overline{JK} \perp \overline{ML}$ and $\overline{MP} \cong \overline{PL}$, then $\overline{JK}$ is a _____.

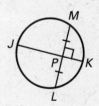

Example 2   *Find the Center of a Circle*

Suppose an archaeologist finds part of a circular plate. Show how to reconstruct the original shape of the plate.

Solution

1. On the diagram at the right, draw any two chords that are not parallel to each other.

2. Draw the perpendicular bisector of each chord. These lines contain diameters.

3. The diameters intersect at the center of the circle. Use a compass to draw the rest of the plate.

Follow-Up

Why does the method in Example 2 work?

THEOREM 11.6

Words In the same circle, or in congruent circles:

• If two chords are congruent, then their
_____ are congruent.

• If two minor arcs are congruent, then their
_____ are congruent.

Symbols If $\overline{AB} \cong \overline{DC}$, then _____ $\cong$ _____ .

If $\overparen{AB} \cong \overparen{DC}$, then _____ $\cong$ _____ .

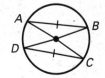

Follow-Up

What is the relationship between the two parts of Theorem 11.6?

Example 3 **Find Measures of Angles and Chords**

Find the value of x.

a.

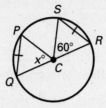

b.

Solution

a. Because $\overline{QP} \cong \overline{RS}$, it follows that $\overparen{QP} \cong \overparen{RS}$.

So, $m\overparen{QP} = m\overparen{RS} = $ ____ °, and $x = $ ____ .

b. Because $\overparen{AB} \cong \overparen{DE}$, it follows that $\overline{AB} \cong \overline{DE}$.

So, $AB = DE = $ ___ , and $x = $ ___ .

✓ *Checkpoint* Find the value of x.

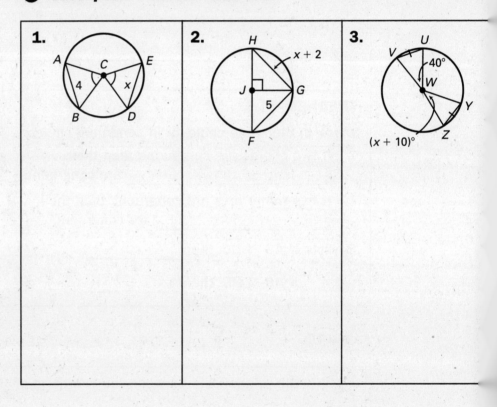

1.	2.	3.

11.5 Inscribed Angles and Polygons

Goal Use properties of inscribed angles.

VOCABULARY

Inscribed angle

Intercepted arc

Inscribed

Circumscribed

THEOREM 11.7: MEASURE OF AN INSCRIBED ANGLE

Words If an angle is inscribed in a circle, then its measure is _____ the measure of its intercepted arc.

Symbols $m\angle ADB = \underline{\quad} \cdot m\widehat{AB}$

Example 1 **Measures of Inscribed Angles and Arcs**

Find the measure of the inscribed angle or the intercepted arc.

a.

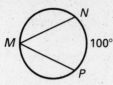

b.

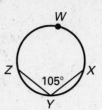

Solution

a. $m\angle NMP = \dfrac{1}{2}$ _____ = _____ = _____

b. _____ $= \dfrac{1}{2}m\overarc{ZWX}$ **Theorem 11.7**

_____ $= \dfrac{1}{2}m\overarc{ZWX}$ **Substitute.**

_____ $= m\overarc{ZWX}$ **Multiply each side by __.**

✓ *Checkpoint* **Find the measure of the inscribed angle or the intercepted arc.**

1.	**2.**	**3.**
	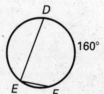	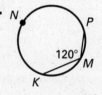

THEOREM 11.8

Words If a triangle inscribed in a circle is a right triangle, then the hypotenuse is _____ of the circle.

If a leg of a triangle inscribed in a circle is a diameter of the circle, then the triangle is a _____ triangle.

Example 2   *Find Angle Measures*

Find the values of *x* and *y*.

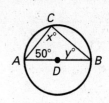

Solution

Because △*ABC* is inscribed in a circle and
$\overline{AB}$ is a diameter, △*ABC* is a right triangle
with hypotenuse $\overline{AB}$. Therefore, *x* = ___ .

Because ∠*A* and ∠*B* are acute angles of a right triangle,
y = 90 − ___ = ___ .

✔ **Checkpoint** Find the values of *x* and *y* in ⊙*C*.

4.	5.	6.

THEOREM 11.9

Words If a quadrilateral can be inscribed
in a circle, then its opposite angles are

_____ .

If the opposite angles of a quadrilateral are
_____ , then the quadrilateral can
be inscribed in a circle.

Example 3 *Find Angle Measures*

Find the values of y and z.

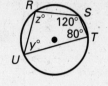

Solution

Because *RSTU* is inscribed in a circle, by Theorem 11.9, opposite angles must be _____.

∠S and ∠U are opposite angles.   ∠R and ∠T are opposite angles

   $m\angle S + m\angle U =$ _____ $m\angle R + m\angle T =$ _____

   _____ + _____ = _____   _____ + _____ = _____

            $y =$ _____ $z =$ _____

Follow-Up

In Example 3, what should the sum of the measures of the interior angles of *RSTU* be?

Check the sum.

✔ *Checkpoint* Find the values of *x* and *y* in ⊙*C*.

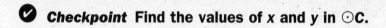

7.

8.

9.

11.6 Properties of Chords

Goal Use properties of chords in a circle.

THEOREM 11.10

Words If two chords intersect inside a circle, then the measure of each angle formed is one half the _____ of the measures of the arcs intercepted by the angle and its vertical angle.

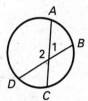

Symbols $m\angle 1 = \dfrac{1}{2}($ _____ $)$,

$m\angle 2 = \dfrac{1}{2}($ _____ $)$

| **Example 1** | **Find the Measure of an Angle** |

Find the value of x.

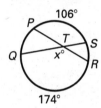

Solution

$x° = \dfrac{1}{2}($ _____ $)$ Use Theorem 11.10.

$x° = \dfrac{1}{2}($ _____ $)$ Substitute.

$x =$ _____   Add.

$x =$ _____   Multiply.

Example 2   *Find the Measure of an Arc*

Find the value of x.

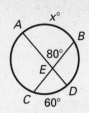

Solution

$m\angle AEB = \dfrac{1}{2}($ _____ + _____ $)$ Use Theorem 11.10.

____ $= \dfrac{1}{2}($ _____ $)$ Substitute.

____ $=$ ____ $+ 30$ Distributive property

____ $=$ ____   Subtract ____ from each side.

____ $=$ ___   Multiply each side by ___.

✔ *Checkpoint* **Find the value of x.**

1.

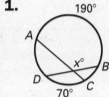

2.

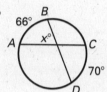

3.

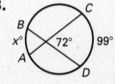

THEOREM 11.11

Words If two chords intersect inside a circle, then the product of the lengths of the segments of one chord is equal to the _____

_____ .

Symbols $EA \cdot EB =$ _____

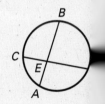

Follow-Up

What is the hypothesis for both Theorems 11.10 and 11.11?

Example 3 *Find Segment Lengths*

Find the value of *x*.

Solution

Notice that $\overline{ST}$ and $\overline{QP}$ are chords that intersect at *R*.

$RS \cdot RT = \underline{\hspace{2cm}}$	Use Theorem 11.11.
$\underline{\hspace{1cm}} = \underline{\hspace{1cm}}$	Substitute.
$\underline{\hspace{1cm}} = \underline{\hspace{1cm}}$	Simplify.
$\underline{\hspace{1cm}} = \underline{\hspace{1cm}}$	Divide each side by __ .

✔ **Checkpoint** Find the value of *x*.

4.	5.	6.

11.7 Equations of Circles

Goal Write and graph the equations of a circle.

Example 1 *Write an Equation of a Circle*

Write an equation of the circle.

Solution

The radius of the circle is ___ . The center is at the _____.

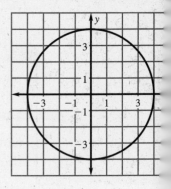

$x^2 + y^2 = r^2$ Equation of a circle

$x^2 + y^2 = (\underline{\ \ })^2$ Substitute.

$x^2 + y^2 = \underline{\ \ \ }$ Simplify.

Answer An equation of the circle is _____ .

✔ *Checkpoint* Write an equation of the circle.

1.

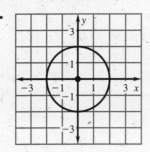

2.

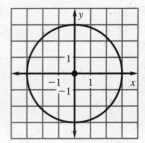

STANDARD EQUATION OF A CIRCLE

In the coordinate plane, the standard equation
of the circle with center at (h, k) and radius r is

$$(x - h)^2 + (y - k)^2 = r^2.$$

The *x*-coordinate of the center is ___ .

The *y*-coordinate of the center is ___ .

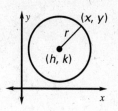

Example 2   *Write the Standard Equation of a Circle*

Write the standard equation of the circle with
center $(2, -1)$ and radius 3.

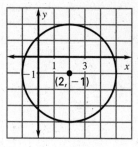

Solution

$$\underline{\hspace{3cm}} = \underline{\hspace{1cm}} \quad \text{Standard equation of a circle}$$

$$\underline{\hspace{3cm}} = \underline{\hspace{1cm}} \quad \text{Substitute.}$$

$$(x - \underline{\ })^2 + (y + \underline{\ })^2 = \underline{\ } \quad \text{Simplify.}$$

Answer The standard equation of the circle is

$$\underline{\hspace{4cm}}.$$

Follow-Up Write the coordinates of the center of the circle with the
given equation.

$(x - 3)^2 + (y + 2)^2 = 1$ _____

$(x + 3)^2 + (y - 2)^2 = 1$ _____

$(x + 3)^2 + (y + 2)^2 = 1$ _____

$(x - 3)^2 + (y - 2)^2 = 1$ _____

Example 3 *Graph a Circle*

Graph the given equation of the circle.

a. $(x - 1)^2 + (y - 2)^2 = 4$ **b.** $(x + 2)^2 + y^2 = 4$

Solution

a. Rewrite the equation of the circle as
$(x - 1)^2 + (y - 2)^2 = \underline{}^2$

The center is (__ , __) and the radius is __.

Graph the circle below.

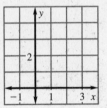

b. Rewrite the equation of the circle as
$(x - \underline{})^2 + (y - \underline{})^2 = \underline{}$

The center is (__ , __) and the radius is __.

Graph the circle below.

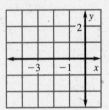

✔ *Checkpoint* **Complete the following exercises.**

3. Write the standard equation of the circle with center $(-4, -6)$ and radius 5.

Graph the given equation of the circle.

4. $(x - 1)^2 + y^2 = 25$

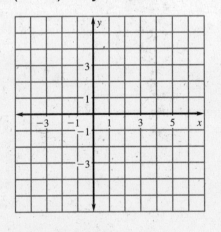

5. $(x + 2)^2 + (y - 4)^2 = 16$

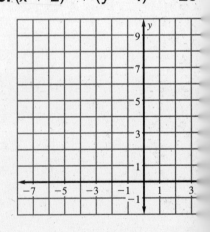

11.8 Rotations

Goal Identify rotations and rotational symmetry.

VOCABULARY

Rotation

Center of rotation

Angle of rotation

Rotational symmetry

Example 1 *Identify Rotational Symmetry*

Does the figure have rotational symmetry? If so, describe the rotations that map the figure onto itself.

a. Rectangle

b. Trapezoid

Solution

a. _____ . A rectangle can be mapped onto itself by a _____ or _____ rotation of _____ ° about its center.

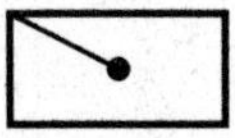

0°    180°

b. _____ . A trapezoid _____ rotational symmetry.

Follow-Up Figures A, B, and C are images of the original figure below. Tell which figure shows the rotation described.

Original figure   Figure A   Figure B   Figure C

90° clockwise rotation _____

180° clockwise rotation _____

180° counterclockwise rotation _____

90° counterclockwise rotation _____

✔ **Checkpoint** Does the figure have rotational symmetry? If so, describe the rotations that map the figure onto itself.

1. Isosceles trapezoid	2. Parallelogram	3. Regular octagon
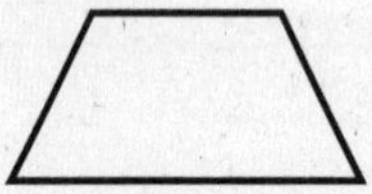	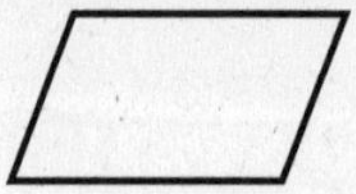	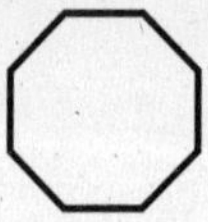

Example 2   *Rotations*

Rotate △*FGH* 50° counterclockwise about point *C*.

Solution

Use a protractor, a compass, and a straightedge.

1. To find the image of point *F*, draw $\overline{CF}$ and draw a 50° angle. Find *F′* so that *CF* = *CF′*.

2. To find the image of point *G*, draw $\overline{CG}$ and draw a 50° angle. Find *G′* so that *CG* = *CG′*.

3. To find the image of point *H*, draw $\overline{CH}$ and draw a 50° angle. Find *H′* so that *CH* = *CH′*. Draw *F′G′H′*.

Example 3   *Rotations in a Coordinate Plane*

Sketch the quadrilateral with vertices *A*(2, −2), *B*(4, 1), *C*(5, 1), and *D*(5, −1). Then, rotate it 90° counterclockwise about the origin and name the coordinates of the new vertices.

Solution

Plot the vertices *A*, *B*, *C*, and *D*. Draw *ABCD*.

Use a protractor, a compass, and a straightedge to find the rotated vertices *A′*, *B′*, *C′*, and *D′*.

The coordinates of the vertices of the image are *A′*(___, ___), *B′*(___, ___), *C′*(___, ___), *D′*(___, ___).

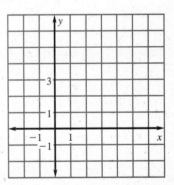

Words to Review

Give an example of the vocabulary word.

Chord, secant, tangent	**Point of tangency**
Tangent segment	**Minor arc, major arc**
Semicircle	**Congruent circles**
Congruent arcs	**Arc length**

Inscribed angle, intercepted arc	Inscribed
Circumscribed	Standard equation of a circle
Rotation	Center of rotation
Angle of rotation	Rotational symmetry

Review your notes and Chapter 11 by using the Chapter Summary and Review on pages 641–645 of your textbook.